THE FUTURE OF UNION ORGANIZING

HEARING

BEFORE THE

SUBCOMMITTEE ON HEALTH, EMPLOYMENT, LABOR, AND PENSIONS

COMMITTEE ON EDUCATION AND THE WORKFORCE

U.S. HOUSE OF REPRESENTATIVES

ONE HUNDRED THIRTEENTH CONGRESS

FIRST SESSION

HEARING HELD IN WASHINGTON, DC SEPTEMBER 19, 2013

Serial No. 113–33

Printed for the use of the Committee on Education and the Workforce

Available via the World Wide Web:
www.gpo.gov/fdsys/browse/committee.action?chamber=house&committee=education or
Committee address: *http://edworkforce.house.gov*

U.S. GOVERNMENT PRINTING OFFICE

82–792 PDF   WASHINGTON : 2014

For sale by the Superintendent of Documents, U.S. Government Printing Office
Internet: bookstore.gpo.gov   Phone: toll free (866) 512–1800; DC area (202) 512–1800
Fax: (202) 512–2104   Mail: Stop IDCC, Washington, DC 20402–0001

COMMITTEE ON EDUCATION AND THE WORKFORCE

JOHN KLINE, Minnesota, *Chairman*

Thomas E. Petri, Wisconsin
Howard P. "Buck" McKeon, California
Joe Wilson, South Carolina
Virginia Foxx, North Carolina
Tom Price, Georgia
Kenny Marchant, Texas
Duncan Hunter, California
David P. Roe, Tennessee
Glenn Thompson, Pennsylvania
Tim Walberg, Michigan
Matt Salmon, Arizona
Brett Guthrie, Kentucky
Scott DesJarlais, Tennessee
Todd Rokita, Indiana
Larry Bucshon, Indiana
Trey Gowdy, South Carolina
Lou Barletta, Pennsylvania
Martha Roby, Alabama
Joseph J. Heck, Nevada
Susan W. Brooks, Indiana
Richard Hudson, North Carolina
Luke Messer, Indiana

George Miller, California,
  Senior Democratic Member
Robert E. Andrews, New Jersey
Robert C. "Bobby" Scott, Virginia
Rubén Hinojosa, Texas
Carolyn McCarthy, New York
John F. Tierney, Massachusetts
Rush Holt, New Jersey
Susan A. Davis, California
Raúl M. Grijalva, Arizona
Timothy H. Bishop, New York
David Loebsack, Iowa
Joe Courtney, Connecticut
Marcia L. Fudge, Ohio
Jared Polis, Colorado
Gregorio Kilili Camacho Sablan,
  Northern Mariana Islands
John A. Yarmuth, Kentucky
Frederica S. Wilson, Florida
Suzanne Bonamici, Oregon

Juliane Sullivan, *Staff Director*
Jody Calemine, *Minority Staff Director*

————

SUBCOMMITTEE ON HEALTH, EMPLOYMENT, LABOR, AND PENSIONS

DAVID P. ROE, Tennessee, *Chairman*

Joe Wilson, South Carolina
Tom Price, Georgia
Kenny Marchant, Texas
Matt Salmon, Arizona
Brett Guthrie, Kentucky
Scott DesJarlais, Tennessee
Larry Bucshon, Indiana
Trey Gowdy, South Carolina
Lou Barletta, Pennsylvania
Martha Roby, Alabama
Joseph J. Heck, Nevada
Susan W. Brooks, Indiana
Luke Messer, Indiana

Robert E. Andrews, New Jersey,
  Ranking Member
Rush Holt, New Jersey
David Loebsack, Iowa
Robert C. "Bobby" Scott, Virginia
Rubén Hinojosa, Texas
John F. Tierney, Massachusetts
Raúl M. Grijalva, Arizona
Joe Courtney, Connecticut
Jared Polis, Colorado
John A. Yarmuth, Kentucky
Frederica S. Wilson, Florida

C O N T E N T S

THE FUTURE OF UNION ORGANIZING

Thursday, September 19, 2013
House of Representatives,
Subcommittee on Health, Employment Labor & Pensions,
Committee on Education and the Workforce,
Washington, D.C.

The subcommittee met, pursuant to call, at 10:07 a.m., in Room 2175, Rayburn House Office Building, Hon. David P. Roe [chairman of the subcommittee] presiding.

Present: Representatives Roe, Salmon, Guthrie, DesJarlais, Andrews, Holt, Grijalva, Courtney, and Wilson.

Also present: Representatives Kline and Miller.

Staff present: Katherine Bathgate, Deputy Press Secretary; Owen Caine, Legislative Assistant; Molly Conway, Professional Staff Member; Ed Gilroy, Director of Workforce Policy; Benjamin Hoog, Senior Legislative Assistant; Marvin Kaplan, Workforce Policy Counsel; Brian Newell, Deputy Communications Director; Krisann Pearce, General Counsel; Molly McLaughlin Salmi, Deputy Director of Workforce Policy; Alissa Strawcutter, Deputy Clerk; Loren Sweatt, Senior Policy Advisor; Aaron Albright, Minority Communications Director for Labor; Tylease Alli, Minority Clerk/Intern and Fellow Coordinator; Jody Calemine, Minority Staff Director; Melissa Greenberg, Minority Staff Assistant; Eunice Ikene, Minority Staff Assistant; Brian Levin, Minority Deputy Press Secretary/New Media Coordinator; Richard Miller, Minority Senior Labor Policy Advisor; Megan O'Reilly, Minority General Counsel; Michele Varnhagen, Minority Chief Policy Advisor/Labor Policy Director; Michael Zola, Minority Deputy Staff Director; and Mark Zuckerman, Minority Senior Economic Advisor.

Chairman ROE. A quorum being present, the Subcommittee on Health, Employment, Labor and Pensions will come to order. This morning we will broadly examine the future of union organizing. It is no secret the number of workers electing to join a union has declined sharply in recent decades. Since 1983, the share of all workers belonging to a union has dropped from roughly 20 percent to less than 12 percent.

Today, fewer than 7 percent of private sector workers are union members. AFL–CIO president, Richard Trumka, recently warned the labor movement is in crisis. Gary Chaison, an industrial relations professor at Clark University, told the New York Times unions are thrashing around looking for answers, and there is a sense that this is a make or break time for labor. Either major changes are done, or we will be too late to resuscitate the labor movement. As union leaders try desperately to swell the ranks of dues-paying members, we have to ensure the tools they use abide by the law and are in the best interests of our workforce.

We must also hold federal agencies accountable for the role they play as union looks to regain the support they once held among America's workers. Toward that end, this committee has repeatedly expressed concerns with the culture of union favoritism embraced by the current administration. In some cases, we have stated our disapproval and called for a course of correction. In others, we have advanced legislation that would strengthen the rights of workers and ensure a level playing field between unions and employers.

Schemes such as ambush elections or micro unions will spark radical changes in the union organizing process. Under the process envisioned by union leaders, a worker's right make to informed decisions in union elections is diminished, employers' freedom to communicate with employees is stifled, and workers' privacy is jeopardized. And the solidarity in the workplace is broken. As a result, it will be virtually impossible for workers to freely vote their conscience. Aside from the help of friendly federal agencies, union leaders are also pursuing inventive strategies to organize workers.

Recent news reports have highlighted one particular strategy to utilize worker centers to build employee support for unionization. Worker centers often engage in traditional union activities, such as corporate campaigns and employee walkouts. But because they operate under the guise of non-profit community organizations, they can avoid a range of federal standards that have long governed union contact. Chairman Klein and I have asked the Department of Labor to clarify the legal obligations of worker centers.

While the response we received to our initial inquiry was incomplete and disappointing, we are hopeful Secretary Perez will provide more substantive answers to our questions. We should support every effort to improve wages and working conditions of those struggling in today's economy, so long as those efforts follow the law. The question of union representation is a deeply personal matter for any worker. It is important to remember what has been, and must remain, the vital principle of federal labor law.

The law is supposed to enable unions to organize every workplace, and the law isn't designed to help employers obstruct union representation. Fundamentally, the law exists to protect the right of workers to freely choose to join or not join a union. Defending this right is the responsibility of every elected policymaker, and this committee will continue to demand fair and objective policies that allow workers to make this important decision without a fear of coercion, intimidation or retribution. And we will work to ensure these policies are vigorously enforced.

Before I close, I want to thank our witnesses for being with us. I would also like to extend a special thanks to Mr. Clarence Adams, a Marine veteran. Mr. Adams was the first of many troops deployed under Operation Iraqi Freedom. This week's senseless tragedy at the Navy Yard reminds us of the sacrifice rendered every day by the men and women in our armed forces. Mr. Adams, we are grateful for you service to our country, and for your participation in today's hearing.

I will now recognize our senior Democratic member of the subcommittee, my colleague, Mr. Andrews, for his opening statement.

[The statement of Chairman Roe follows:]

Prepared Statement of Hon. Phil Roe, Chairman, Subcommittee on Health, Employment, Labor, and Pensions

This morning we will broadly examine the future of union organizing. It's no secret the number of workers electing to join a union has declined sharply in recent decades. Since 1983 the share of all workers belonging to a union has dropped from roughly 20 percent to less than 12 percent. Today fewer than seven percent of private-sector workers are union members.

AFL–CIO President Richard Trumka recently warned the labor movement is in a "crisis." Gary Chaison, an industrial relations professor at Clark University, told the *New York Times,* "Unions are thrashing around looking for answers. There's a sense that this is make-or-break time for labor. Either major things are done, or it will be too late to resuscitate the labor movement."

As union leaders try desperately to swell the ranks of dues-paying members, we have to ensure the tools they use abide by the law and are in the best interests of our workforce. We also must hold federal agencies accountable for the role they play as unions look to regain the support they once held among America's workers.

Toward that end, this committee has repeatedly expressed concerns with the culture of union favoritism embraced by the current administration. In some cases, we have stated our disapproval and called for a course correction. In others, we have advanced legislation that would strengthen the rights of workers and ensure a level playing field between unions and employers.

Schemes such as ambush elections and micro-unions will spark radical changes in the union organizing process. Under the process envisioned by union leaders, workers' right to make informed decisions in union elections is diminished; employers' freedom to communicate with employees is stifled; workers' privacy is jeopardized; and solidarity in the workplace is broken. As a result, it will be virtually impossible for workers to freely vote their conscience.

Aside from the help of friendly federal agencies, union leaders are also pursuing inventive strategies to organize workers. Recent news reports have highlighted one particular strategy to utilize worker centers to build employee support for unionization. Worker centers often engage in traditional union activities, such as corporate campaigns and employee walkouts. But because they operate under the guise of nonprofits community organizations, they can avoid a range of federal standards that have long governed union conduct.

Chairman Kline and I have asked the Department of Labor to clarify the legal obligations of worker centers. While the response we received to our initial inquiry was incomplete and disappointing, we are hopeful Secretary Perez will provide more substantive answers to our questions. We should support every effort to help improve the wages and working conditions of those struggling in today's economy, so long as those efforts follow the law.

The question of union representation is a deeply personal matter for any worker. It is important to remember what has been and must remain the vital principle of federal labor law. The law isn't supposed to enable unions to organize every workplace. And the law isn't designed to help employers obstruct union representation. Fundamentally the law exists to protect the right of workers to freely choose to join or not join a union.

Defending this right is the responsibility of every elected policymaker, and this committee will continue to demand fair and objective policies that allow workers to make this important decision without fear of coercion, intimidation, and retribution, and we will work to ensure these policies are vigorously enforced.

Before I close, I want to thank our witnesses for being with us. I'd also like to extend a special thanks to Mr. Clarence Adams. As a marine veteran, Mr. Adams was the first of many troops deployed under Operation Iraqi Freedom. This week's senseless tragedy at the Navy Yard reminds us of the sacrifice rendered every day by the men and women in our Armed Forces. Mr. Adams, we are grateful for your service to our country and for your participation in today's hearing.

I will now recognize the senior Democratic member of the subcommittee, my colleague Mr. Andrews, for his opening remarks.

———

Mr. ANDREWS. Thank you, Mr. Chairman. I would also like to thank the witnesses for their diligence in preparation for today's hearing. We are glad that you are here. And I thank you, Mr. Chairman, for starting this hearing off with a solemn reminder of those who lost their lives working for our country just a few blocks from here, at the Navy Yard, on Monday. We are deeply in their debt, and I appreciate you honoring their service with your remarks this morning.

When I was home for our extended break in August and early September, I got the sense from listening to a lot of constituents that although the economy has improved certainly since the dark days of 5 years ago, when the economy nearly collapsed, that it is not good enough. It has just not gained the traction that we need to lift people out of the struggles that they feel every day. Now, one way to—one thing we should certainly not do is continue with the budget sequester policies that, unfortunately, this House is gonna vote to renew either tomorrow or Friday.

I hope that we can find a way to reenergize our economy by reducing and eliminating the sequester. But one thing we should do is regenerate the middle class. Our economy works when a middle class worker gets her kitchen remodeled. Because the kitchen remodeler then is likely to go out and buy a car. And the car salesman earns more commissions, so he or she is more likely to buy a house. And the real estate agent earns a commission, so he or she is more likely to go out to a restaurant. And the owner of the restaurant is more likely to hire more servers and more workers and they are more likely to get their kitchens remodeled. And on it goes.

So we believe that you grow the economy from the middle class out. There has been an unhappy story, even in this recovery, for the middle class. In the early days of this economic recovery, for every 1 dollar of growth that went to higher wages for America's workers $70 went to corporate profits in the country. So by a 70-to-1 ratio the benefits of growth that we have seen have gone to corporate profits and not to employee wages. What do you do about that?

Well, the evidence broadly suggests that when people engage in collective bargaining that those results are considerably better. On the average, members of unions earn 27 percent more than those who don't belong to a union for similar work. Members of unions are 28 percent more likely to have health care benefits provided for them at work. They are 64 percent more likely to have a pension plan when they retire. These are the elements of middle class success. This is particularly relevant to groups in our society who have historically suffered under greater burdens and had more difficulty in achieving the American dream.

For African-Americans, African-American workers who are in unions have a median wage that is 30 percent higher than those who are not. For Latinos in our country, Latinos who are in a union have a median wage 58.5 percent higher than those who are not. I think the Chairman exactly stated the intention of U.S. labor law, which is an aggressive neutrality. It is the idea that people should be free to make their own decisions about what is right for them. I certainly agree that that means that there shouldn't be any coercive behavior toward employers or toward employees who do not wish to join a union. Certainly that is part of the law.

And the chairman states it well when he says, and I am quoting him, ''The law is not designed to enable employers to obstruct union representation.'' He is absolutely right. When Mr. Adams came home from Iraq, he went to work for an employer in New

York City and he was part of an effort to organize his fellow workers under the Communication Workers of America. They succeeded, on January 26 of 2012, to win a representation election. Today, all these days later, they still do not have a first contract.

So one of the issues we should be looking at, as we try to grow the economy, grow the middle class and permit those who have freely chosen to join a union and have the benefits of collective bargaining, is, what is happening across this country with those first contracts. I look forward to our discussion here this morning.

I thank the Chairman and look forward to hearing from the witnesses.

Chairman ROE. Thank you, Mr. Andrews.

Pursuant to committee rule 7–C, the members will be permitted to submit written statements to be included in the permanent hearing record. And without objection, the hearing record will remain open for 14 days to allow such statements and other extraneous material referenced during the hearing to be submitted for the official hearing record.

It is now my pleasure to introduce our distinguished panel of witnesses. Mr. Ronald Meisburg is partner of Proskauer Rose in Washington, D.C. Mr. Meisburg served as general counsel for the NLRB for the 4 years, and is a board member for 1 year. And I did a little research on him. He graduated from Carson-Newman College, very close to my home. Welcome.

Mr. David Burton is the general counsel for the National Small Business Association and is testifying on their behalf. Mr. Clarence Adams, a field technician for Cablevision in Brooklyn, New York. Welcome. Mr. Stefan Marculewicz is a shareholder in Littler Mendelson, PC of Washington, D.C.

And before I recognize you to provide your testimony, let me briefly explain our lighting system. You have 5 minutes to present your testimony. When you begin, the light in front of you will turn green. When one minute is left, the light will turn yellow. When your time is expired the light will turn red. At that point, I will ask you to wrap up your remarks as best as you are able. And I won't cut you off in the middle of your remarks, but try to finish up. After everyone has testified, members will each 5 minutes to ask questions.

And right now, I would like to thank the witnesses. And if you would, Mr. Meisburg?

STATEMENT OF MR. RON MEISBURG, MEMBER OF THE FIRM, PROSKAUER, WASHINGTON, D.C.

Mr. MEISBURG. Good morning, Mr. Chairman, members of the subcommittee. My name is Ronald Meisburg. I am a partner in the Proskauer Rose law firm. I am co-chair of the firm's labor-management relations practice group. I appreciate the opportunity to appear before you here today.

My testimony is solely my own. I am not here representing my firm, its clients or any person or organization. I have practiced law now for 39 years. I began my legal career in 1974 in the office of the solicitor of labor; first, in the division of employee benefits, and then the division of mine safety and health. I moved to private practice in 1980, and for the next 23 years I practiced principally in the area of labor relations, including collective bargaining, contract administration, grievance and arbitration proceedings and cases before the NLRB and in federal court.

In 2003, I was nominated for a seat on the National Labor Relations Board by President George W. Bush. I served a recess appointment on the board for 1 year, January through December, 2004. In January 2006 I received a recess appointment for the post of general counsel. I was confirmed by the Senate in August of 2006, and I served as general counsel until mid-2010. Following that, I returned to the private practice of law, where I am now.

I have submitted written testimony about what I see as the areas of law and legal issues that will most likely be addressed by the board in the upcoming months, and I will touch only lightly on them here. In 2011, the board proposed regulations making substantial changes in the representation election process. Some of the proposed regulations that were promulgated were eventually set aside, and are currently pending on appeal in the United States Court of Appeals for the District of Columbia Circuit. Other parts of the proposed regulations have yet to be promulgated.

I would expect the board to revisit that and to attempt to complete what it began in 2011. Many in the management community, I believe, felt that the board's previous rulemaking efforts were not necessary, given the overall success of the board's handling of representation cases. At the time the proposed rules were announced, the board's general counsel had described the board's representation case handling results as outstanding. If the board, in fact, goes forward with further rulemaking it will hopefully follow a process that involves stakeholders earlier—perhaps through an advanced notice of proposed rulemaking—and which focuses on the potential delay caused in outlier cases.

We have also recently seen the board expand in areas of concerted protected activity, such as decisions addressing non-employee and off-duty employee access to an employer's property and protection from employee social media statements. I would expect the board to continue to expand these areas and the concept of protected activity, particularly as it is adapted to developments in the organization of work and the revolution we are seeing in technology. And I would hope that the board does this with a sense of balance, recognizing that the NLRA is one of a constellation of federal, state and local workplace laws with which employers must comply.

I also expect the board will continue to apply, and perhaps refine, its tests for the determination of bargaining units announced in specialty health care through both administrative processes at the regional office level, as well as cases coming before the board itself. And the board will continue to deal with the fallout from the recess appointment issue in many cases where it has been raised, both with respect to the board and with respect to some of the regional directors and also delegations of the board. And just a few weeks ago, there was a decision by a federal district court in Washington which held the general counsel's appointment in 2010, under the Federal Vacancies Reform Act, to have been invalid.

So the board and its staff, unfortunately, are going to be distracted by a lot of these cases as they go forward. Finally, let me say a brief word about the career staff at the board with whom I had the pleasure of working on almost a daily basis for several years. They serve the appointees like a lawyer serves a client: giving advice, speaking directly, arguing their points. But when a decision is made, they turn to delivering a draft opinion or advice memorandum, or brief or other action as decided by the appointee. And they do this whether they serve a Republican appointee or a Democrat appointee.

I have great respect for these career professionals and the staff that supports them, and I hope they can be kept free of the political crossfire that sometimes engulfs the NLRB. Thank you very much for this time, and I look forward to your questions.

[The statement of Mr. Meisburg follows:]

TESTIMONY OF RONALD MEISBURG
PARTNER, PROSKAUER ROSE LLP

What to Look for from the New NLRB
U.S. House Committee on Education and the Workforce Subcommittee on Health,
Employment, Labor, and Pensions

September 19, 2013, 10:00 a.m.

Mr. Chairman, Members of the Subcommittee, I am delighted to appear before you today. My name is Ronald Meisburg. I practice law as a partner at Proskauer Rose LLP. I am co-chair of the firm's Labor Management Relations practice group. My testimony is solely my own and I do not represent my firm, its clients or any other person or organization.

I began my legal career in 1974 in the Office of the Solicitor of Labor. For six years, I served in the Division of Employee Benefits and then in the Division of Mine Safety and Health. While I was there, I was a member of a litigation team that won the Secretary of Labor's Distinguished Achievement Award. I moved to private practice in 1980 and for the next 23 years spent most of my time representing management in various aspects of labor relations, including collective bargaining, contract administration, grievance and arbitration proceedings, and cases before the NLRB and the federal courts.

In late 2003, President George W. Bush selected me as his nominee for a seat on the National Labor Relations Board, and I served a recess appointment as a Board Member from January through December, 2004. I next served as a Special Assistant to NLRB General Counsel Arthur Rosenfeld during 2005, and in January, 2006, I received my second recess appointment – this one to the post of NLRB General Counsel. While serving as a recess appointee, I was confirmed by the Senate in August, 2006, and served until June, 2010, as a confirmed General Counsel.

Following my service at the NLRB I returned to the private practice of labor law.

I have been asked to testify regarding what I see as areas of law and legal issues that will most likely be addressed by the Board in the upcoming months. While the Board's agenda is set partly by what cases are brought to the Board, it is also a function of what issues in those cases the Board and the General Counsel want to emphasize, either by refining, broadening, narrowing or overruling prior precedent. Also, recently the Board has turned to rule making to flesh out its agenda in areas not as easily addressed in the cases.

Representation Election Regulations: I expect that the Board will want to take some action to get its effort to revise its representation election rules back on track. The Board issued a notice of proposed rulemaking in June, 2011. 76 FR 36812 (June 22, 2011). Written and oral testimony was accepted in July and August, and thousands of comments from labor and management representatives and academics were received by the Board. In December, 2011, a portion of the proposed regulations was putatively promulgated, while a portion of them was reserved for future action. 76 FR 80138 (December 22, 2011).

However, a federal district court in the District of Columbia held that only two of the three sitting Board members had participated in the rule's promulgation, and set the regulations aside on that basis. *Chamber of Commerce of the United States of America et al. v. NLRB*, 879 F. Supp. 2d 18 (D.D.C. 2012) *motion to alter or amend den'd* (July 27, 2012). The district court's decision was appealed to the U.S. Court of Appeals for the District of Columbia Circuit, where it is currently pending. *Chamber of Commerce of the United States et al. v. NLRB*, No. 12-5250 (August 7, 2012).

Following the D.C. Circuit's decision in *Noel Canning v. NLRB*, 705 F.3d 490 (D.C. Cir. 2013) (holding the President's January 4, 2012 recess appointments of NLRB Members Block and Griffin were invalid because they did not occur during an inter-session recess of the

Senate, and were not for a vacancy which arose during such inter-session recess), the respondents in the *Chamber of Commerce* case asserted another ground for invalidating the regulations – that one of the two members who had promulgated the rule was himself unlawfully appointed, and therefore the rules were invalidly promulgated by only one Board member. The D.C. Circuit has now ordered this case held in abeyance pending the decision of the Supreme Court in *Noel Canning*.

In the meantime, the Chairman of the Board has indicated that he wishes to move forward with those parts of the proposed rule that were not promulgated in December, 2011. Daily Labor Report 2013 Labor Outlook, "NLRB Determined to Act in Year of Challenges" (at pg. S-23), *found at* http://op.bna.com/dlrcases.nsf/id/smgk-94ns5v/$File/dlr2013laboroutlook.pdf . But that desire seems to assume that the earlier putatively promulgated rules would be in force. Now, because of the D.C. Circuit *Chamber of Commerce* litigation and the pendency of the *Noel Canning* case in the Supreme Court, that supposition is in substantial doubt and it will not likely be resolved for many months. So how does the Board move forward under these circumstances?

At the outset, it should be noted that in general the employer community did not see and does not see the need for the Board to move forward with these regulations. The existing election procedures work well. At the time of the rulemaking, the Board's statistics showed that all Board elections were held within 38 median days from the filing of an election petition. And 95% of all elections were held within 56 days.

Further, the proposed rules contain substantive changes that are ill conceived. For example, there is an effective seven day deadline following the filing of a petition for holding a representation hearing. This was coupled with a requirement that the employer produce a pre-hearing position statement on or before the hearing date. Failure to raise an issue in the position statement would be deemed a waiver of the issue. This was seen as an unfair denial of rights and highly prejudicial to businesses, particularly small businesses that may not have the ability to engage legal counsel and prepare a proper and thorough position statement.

These and many other issues of concern to employers were addressed in comments that I helped prepare for the U.S. Chamber of Commerce. These comments were submitted to the Board and can be found at http://www.regulations.gov/#!documentDetail;D=NLRB-2011-0002-51430.

Assuming the Board moves forward, it will have to deal with the part of the regulation it attempted to promulgate but which is hung up in litigation in the D.C. Circuit. Should the Board wish to proceed, it will have to determine whether to proceed piecemeal with the remaining proposed regulations that were not previously promulgated; or to withdraw the previously promulgated rules and seek dismissal of the D.C. Circuit appeal. Following the latter course would allow the Board to start the entire process over, and perhaps the rulemaking would be more focused, for example, on the causes of delay in outlier cases, which appear to represent 5% or less of the Board's election case load.

If undertaken, this new start could include doing something suggested by many commentators, and that is, issuance of an advanced notice of proposed rulemaking that could be informally evaluated by interested parties. The Board is fortunate in that it gets lots of opportunities for informal feedback from its various constituencies, whether through the ABA Committee meetings that it regularly attends, or on the speaking circuit where Board members typically address groups of employment and union lawyers before various local bar groups. If a pre-proposal draft were shared with the public, and sufficient time were given for study of that draft, this informal process could allow the Board to receive valuable input that could be taken into account in any formally proposed rule, and, indeed, in deciding whether any proposed rule were necessary.

Protected Concerted Activity: I also expect the Board to continue to expand what constitutes protected concerted activity. It is difficult to understate the reaction of employers to the series of cases in which the Board has broken new ground in defining what constitutes protected concerted activity. Many of the cases involve new and evolving technology and new ways of organizing work. For example, the Board's efforts to protect social media posts that meet the test for concerted activity came as a big surprise to many employers. The Acting General Counsel has been quoted as saying that conversations on social media are no different than those around a water cooler. It may be true in some cases that comments on social media may have replaced, or augmented, protected water cooler conversations. And to that extent, they may be protected.

But the Board may not appreciate the extent to which these social media postings and conversations on the internet have the potential to cause much unjustified harm to an employer. Many of them take place outside the work environment, which is to be expected given the ubiquity of home computers and the portability of smart phones and other mobile devices which can provide access to the internet almost anywhere. For that reason, employee comments may sometimes be less measured and perhaps more careless than they might be if made face to face in the presence of co-workers. But whatever the reason, these comments can be very sharply and perhaps unfairly critical of employers and supervisors and managers. Worse, unlike the water cooler conversations, they are published to perhaps millions of people, most or all of whom are not co-workers, in effectively a permanent form with unlimited distribution.

So I would hope to see the NLRB take this into account when evaluating and deciding these cases. The Board has developed standards for when employee statements may lose the protection of the Act. Just as the Board is updating the meaning of protected activity to account for new technologies, it should also update the standards for when employee comments may lose the protection of the Act when made on social media, taking into account the difference between statements made on the internet and statements made around the water cooler.

We already have in the common law an historical distinction between libel and slander. Libel traditionally has been treated more seriously because of the relative permanence and distributable nature of written libel as opposed to spoken slander. Technological advances have made the distinction less clear, principally because of audio and video recordings of spoken slander have made it more like traditional libel. Perhaps the Board can take a cue from this in developing a coherent body of law which protects, within balanced and reasonable limits, the relatively permanent and highly distributable social media speech on the internet.

Interference, Restraint and Coercion: Another area where the Board will continue to address and expand is what constitutes employer interference, restraint and coercion with respect to such activities. For example, the Board has held that an employer may not give a blanket confidentiality instruction to employees during an investigation into a workplace incident. *E.g., Banner Health System*, 358 NLRB No. 93 (July 30, 2012). The basis for this is that a blanket rule requiring confidentiality may chill the right of an employee to consult with a fellow employee or a third party regarding the investigation.

I am told by my colleagues who do such investigations that confidentiality instructions are routine, and serve the purpose of not only protecting the integrity of the investigation, but also of protecting the identity of complainants who may otherwise be reluctant to come forward, and the identity of persons who may be wrongfully accused, before the investigation can be completed and appropriate action taken by the employer.

I think it is important to note that these workplace investigations involve all sorts of incidents that do not arise under the NLRA. Typically they will involve whistle blowing, or accusations of harassment, discrimination, theft, vandalism, or other types of work place conduct or incidents. The ability of the employer to fully investigate them is important to carrying out the protections and policies under other federal, state and local laws, where confidentiality is needed. Indeed, I am told by my colleagues who do EEO investigations that the EEOC urges confidentiality in investigations.

To be clear, the NLRB has not outlawed all confidentiality instructions. But it has required the employer to *first* make a determination that failure to give the confidentiality instruction will likely result in the falsification of testimony, the fabrication of evidence, the intimidation of other witnesses, or some similar justification. The problems with this are several-fold. First, what is the process for making such a determination? Second, how can such a determination be made without talking to witnesses on a non-confidential basis, thus potentially rendering any later confidentiality instruction nugatory? And third, will the delays engendered through making the determination delay the investigation and put an accurate outcome at risk?

In a sense, this is an overarching problem with the Board's jurisprudence in this area. While it is possible to look at a rule or at a particular practice and clearly see how it might chill the assertion of protected rights, sometimes the Board delves too far into the theoretical.

The Board's recent decisions on return to work policies for off duty employees serve as an example. *E.g., J. W. Marriot Los Angeles at L.A. Live,* 359 NLRB No. 8 (September 28, 2012). Essentially the Board holds that if a return to work policy allows the employer any discretion whatsoever in allowing an off duty employee back onto the property, then the rule is unlawful. The basis for this is that if an employee has to ask permission to go back to meet another employee on some union business, or engage in the protected activity of a meeting to discuss work conditions, the employee may be chilled in asking for permission.

But this throws the baby out with the bath water because it also keeps an employee who needs to go back to retrieve some property left in his locker or some other non-labor related reason from having a flexible rule where his employer can say yes. In these types of cases, the Board should be more willing to wait for an actual instance of alleged wrongdoing, rather than preclude a common sense rule that may be fairly and legally administered by an employer.

Access to and Use of Property: Another issue that the Board will be dealing with is non-employee access to an employer's property. In *Roundy's Inc.,* the Board invited *amicus* briefs on the following questions:

1. In cases alleging unlawful employer discrimination in
nonemployee access, should the Board continue to apply the
standard articulated by the Board majority in Sandusky Mall Co., above?
2. If not, what standard should the Board adopt to define
discrimination in this context?
3. What bearing, if any, does Register Guard, 351 NLRB 1110
(2007), enf. denied in part 571 F.3d 53 (D.C. Cir. 2009), have
on the Board's standard for finding unlawful discrimination in
nonemployee access cases?

Case 30-CA-17185 (Notice and Invitation to File Briefs, November 12, 2010).

The Board's likely purpose in this is to resolve a seeming inconsistency in Board law involving what constitutes discrimination in access to or use of an employer's property by employees and non-employees, some of whom may be engaged in union activity, while others may be engaged in various forms of commercial and noncommercial/charitable activity.

In *Sandusky Mall,* 329 NLRB 618 (1999), *enf. denied sub nom.,* 242 F.3d 682 (6th Cir. 2001), the Board did not draw any such distinctions and held that it was unlawful discrimination to deny access to or use of an employer's property by non-employees engaged in union activities, while allowing other non-employees access to or use of the property, regardless of the commercial or noncommercial nature of the activities of the other employees.

In *Register Guard,* the Board recognized a distinction between allowing commercial as opposed to noncommercial or charitable use of an employer's email system by employees, and held that denial of use of the email for union business was not discriminatory if no other commercial uses were allowed, either.

The outcome of the *Roundy's* case is awaited with great anticipation, as it has been pending at the Board for over two and one-half years since the completion of briefing.

Specialty Healthcare: The Board will continue to apply, and perhaps refine, its test for the determination of bargaining units announced in Specialty Healthcare, both through the administrative process at the regional level as well as in cases coming before the Board. Chief among the cases awaiting decision at the Board are *Macy's, Inc.,* Case No. 01-RC-091163, and *The Neiman Marcus Group, Inc., d/b/a Bergdorf Goodman,* Case No. 02-RC-076954, both presenting the issue whether employees of a particular department (cosmetics and women's shoes, respectively) may constitute an appropriate bargaining unit, as a departure from the

Board's prior practice of presuming that "wall to wall" units are appropriate in such retail establishments.

The Specialty Healthcare decision was recently upheld in the U.S. Court of Appeals for the Sixth Circuit, *Kindred Nursing Centers East f/k/a Specialty Healthcare v. NLRB*, __ F.3d __, Nos. 12-1027 and 12-1174 (August 15, 2013). Another federal appellate court was presented with, but specifically did not reach, the validity of *Specialty Healthcare*. Instead, the court denied enforcement to the Board's order on the basis that it was issued by an invalid Board, following the reasoning in the *Noel Canning* decision. *Huntington Ingalls Incorporated v. NLRB*, __ F.3d __, Nos. 12-2000 and 12-2065 (July 17, 2013). *See also Nestle Dryer's Ice Cream Co. v. NLRB*, No. 12-1684 (L) (pending on company's motion for summary decision on the recess appointment issue). The issue is likely to be presented in other cases, however, as the NLRB regional offices continue to apply the *Specialty Healthcare* test.

There are sure to be many other issues that will dot the Board's legal landscape in the coming months and years. Among them will be the continuing fall-out from the Recess Appointment issue in the many cases where that has been raised both with respect to the Board itself and with respect to Regional Directors and other officers appointed by the Board. Added to this, just few weeks ago, there was a decision from a federal district court in Washington state which held the Acting General Counsel's appointment to have been unlawful. So the NLRB and its staff will continue to have these distractions to contend with as well.

Finally, I want to say a few words about the Board as an institution. I regard my service as a Board Member and as General Counsel as the honor of a lifetime. On a daily basis I worked with and got to know well members of the agency's career staff. We met and considered some of the most interesting and sometimes vexing issues that continue to arise under the NLRA.

While there may be sharp differences of opinion on certain issues, those cases are the exception and there is broad consensus on many matters.

The career attorneys serve the appointees like any lawyer should serve his or her client – giving advice, speaking directly, arguing their points – and then, when a decision is made, turning to delivering a draft opinion, or advice memorandum, or brief, or other action as it had been decided by the appointee. And this they did whether they served a Republican appointee or a Democrat appointee. In short, I have great respect for these career employees, both professional and support staff, and I appreciate their efforts. And I hope that they can be kept out of the political crossfire accompanying the occasional disputes between the political appointees they work for.

Chairman ROE. Thank you, Mr. Meisburg.
Mr. Burton?

STATEMENT OF MR. DAVID R. BURTON, GENERAL COUNSEL, NATIONAL SMALL BUSINESS ASSOCIATION, WASHINGTON, D.C.

Mr. BURTON. I appreciate the opportunity to be here today. My name is David Burton. I am general counsel for the National Small Business Association. NSBA was founded in 1937, and represents approximately 65,000 small businesses throughout the country. About 28 percent of our members have 20 or more employees. Roughly 4 percent of our members have unions. Roughly 8 percent of our members have dealt with unionization campaigns. And a very large proportion of our members are subject to NLRB jurisdictional standards.

I will quickly address four issues. The DOL has proposed a rule that would radically narrow the advice exemption in the Labor-Management and Disclosure Act and jettison the interpretation of that exemption that has been adopted by every administration since the Kennedy administration. It is our considered view that the proposed rules be withdrawn because it is contrary to congressional intent for at least five reasons.

It upends a century of settled law and creates uncertainty, and imposes dramatically higher costs than the DOL claimed in their estimate; to harm the right of employers to secure advice that will violate the attorney-client privilege; and it lacks an adequate evidentiary basis. For half a century, advisors that did not interact with employees generally did not have to file reports with DOL. In contrast, under the interpretation of section 203–C contained in the proposed rule, virtually any imaginable activity by almost any consultant or vendor that, in any manner, directly or indirectly relates to a labor dispute or attempted organization of an employer would be reportable.

In addition, attorneys, employee benefits consultants and other human resources advisors would probably be reportable. Even extremely minor activities would have to be reported. And if you go back and look at the legislative history, the 1959 conference committee report explicitly stated that Congress intended for the advice exception to be broad. It is, however, difficult to conceive of a more narrowly drafted definition of advice than that contained in the proposed rule.

The proposed rule is inconsistent with basic rules of statutory construction. It more or less reads the 203–C exemption out of the law. It is impermissible to read a section of the statute as unnecessary or meaningless surplusage when an alternative construction can give meaning to the provision. Congress has acquiesced to the definition established by the Kennedy—or the interpretation that satisfied the Kennedy administration for over half a century. That is strong evidence that the Kennedy administration DOL got it right.

The proposed rule also applies to multi-employer seminars, Webinars and conferences. And absent mind-reading skills, the sponsors of those seminars aren't going to know to what use the information is gonna be put. So they will end up having to report on every attendee of their conferences with respect to the fees and who attended. With respect to union elections, in June of 2011 the NLRB published a proposed rule, now withdrawn but likely to be revisited now that the NLRB has a quorum.

The rule would revise election procedures so that in many cases, if not most, elections would be conducted within 10 to 21 days rather than the 35 to 40 days typical today. The members of this committee know a thing or two about elections, and I invite each member of this committee to engage in a thought experiment. Imagine if your opponent was permitted to organize his or her campaign, raise money, hire consultants, recruit volunteers, communicate with voters and only then you were informed there was gonna be an election and it was gonna be in 10 days.

Perhaps I am wrong, but I think most people would regard that as unfair. It is equally unfair in the case of union elections. Small businesses are not familiar with labor law, they don't have labor lawyers on staff. They need time to find advice and to decide how to deal with the potential unionization campaign. In the case of micro unions, we basically are extremely concerned with the line of cases inaugurated by specialty health care.

The case that I think is most notable is the Bergdorf Goodman case, where the second and fifth floor ladies shoe departments were separately organized. When you get into a case where you can organize separate shoe departments in a store, you have the potential to have an incredible multiplicity of bargaining units, tremendous complexity and a balkanization of the workplace.

And with that, I will wrap up my statement. I am glad to answer any questions.

[The statement of Mr. Burton follows:]

National Small Business Association®

TESTIMONY OF DAVID R. BURTON[1]

GENERAL COUNSEL OF

THE NATIONAL SMALL BUSINESS ASSOCIATION

before the

House Committee on Education and the Workforce

Subcommittee on Health, Employment, Labor, and Pensions

regarding

"The Future of Union Organizing,"

September 19, 2013

---

[1] 1156 15th St., NW, Suite 1100, Washington, DC 20005; (202) 296-8830; DBurton@nsba.biz.

22

The NSBA was founded in 1937 to advocate for the interests of small businesses in the U.S. It is the oldest small business organization in the U.S. The NSBA represents more than 65,000 small businesses throughout the country in virtually all industries and of widely varying sizes.

About 28 percent of our members have 20 or more employees. Roughly four percent of our members have unions and 8 percent have dealt with a unionization campaign.[2] A very large proportion of our members fall within National Labor Relations Board (NLRB) jurisdictional standards.[3]

This testimony address four issues:

1. The proposed Department of Labor (DOL) persuader or advice rule;
2. The withdrawn NLRB accelerated union elections rule;
3. NLRB Micro-union or micro-unit decisions; and
4. NLRB social media decisions.

Persuader Rule

On June 21, 2011 the DOL proposed a rule[4] that would make substantial changes to the existing interpretation of the "advice" exemption of the Labor-Management Reporting and Disclosure Act of 1959 (LMRDA)[5] contained in section 203(c) of the Act. The underlying section 203(a)(4) rule imposing reporting obligations is often referred to as the "persuader" rule or the persuader reporting obligations.

It is our considered view that the proposed rule:

- is contrary to Congressional intent (for at least five reasons);
- upends a half century of settled law, creates uncertainty and replaces a relatively clear bright line rule with one riddled with ambiguity;
- imposes substantially higher costs than the DOL claims;
- will harm employers' right to secure advice;
- violates attorney-client privilege; and
- lacks an adequate evidentiary basis.

We have therefore urged the Department to withdraw the proposed rule. The rule has remained unpromulgated since it was proposed over two years ago. DOL has indicated to OMB that it presently expects to finalize the rule by November of this year.

[2] See 2013 NSBA *Workforce and Immigration Study* available at http://nsba.biz/docs/Workforce-Immigration-Survey-2013.pdf .
[3] See NLRB "Jurisdictional Standards," available at http://www.nlrb.gov/rights-we-protect/jurisdictional-standards.
[4] "Labor-Management Reporting and Disclosure Act; Interpretation of the "Advice" Exemption." Proposed Rule, *Federal Register*, Volume 76, Number 119, June 21, 2011, pages 36177-36230. RIN 1215-AB79 and 1245-AA03.
[5] 29 USC 401 *et seq.*

Background

Section 203 of the LMRDA requires employers to report with respect to five different types of matters. Section 203(a)(4) requires that employers report to DOL for public release the details of agreements or arrangements with consultants that undertake persuader activities. The reports are made on DOL-required forms, Form LM-10 and Form LM-20.

Persuader activities are activities "where an object thereof, directly or indirectly, is to persuade employees to exercise or not to exercise, or persuade employees as to the manner of exercising, the right to organize and bargain collectively through representatives of their own choosing, or undertakes to supply such employer with information concerning the activities of employees or a labor organization in connection with a labor dispute involving such employer."[6]

Section 203(c) of the LMRDA provides an exception from the forgoing reporting requirement. The exception covers agreements or arrangements for "advice" and for representing "such employer before any court, administrative agency, or tribunal of arbitration or engaging or agreeing to engage in collective bargaining on behalf of such employer." Ever since a 1962 Kennedy Administration interpretation by the DOL known as the Donahue memorandum (and subsequent formal guidance), the section 203(c) advice exception has been interpreted such that employers and consultants need not file reports when the consultants have no direct contact with employees and act only through the employer who has the choice whether or not to accept and use the advice.[7] Engaging in persuader activity for one client can, however, trigger reporting with respect to other "advice only" clients that would not otherwise be reportable.[8] This has also been the DOL position in litigation and the DOL position has prevailed in court.[9] In other words, when the consultant's role was advisory, no reporting was required. Only when the consultant's role was to actually engage in persuasion was reporting required.

In contrast, under the interpretation of section 203(c) contained in the proposed rule, virtually any imaginable activity by almost any consultant or vendor that in any manner, directly or indirectly, relates to a labor dispute or attempted organization of an employer would be reportable. At the very least, speechwriting, public relations advice, strategic advice, and the preparation of campaign materials, letters, videos, web sites, emails or other materials for employer communication to employees must be reported. As discussed in more detail below, it is also quite likely that employee benefits consultants and similar human resources type advisors will be required to report.[10] There is no de minimis rule based on time or fees. Thus, even extremely minor activities must be reported.

Under the proposed rule, "[t]he duty to report can be triggered even without direct contact between a lawyer or other consultant and employees, if persuading employees is an object, direct

---

[6] Section 203(a)(4) of LMRDA; 29 USC 433(a)(4).

[7] See section 265.005 of the LMRDA Interpretative Manual.

[8] *Master Printers Association v. Donovan*, 699 F.2d 370 (7th Cir.1983), cert. denied, 464 U.S. 1040, 104 S.Ct. 703, 79 L.Ed.2d 168 (1984)

[9] See, e.g., *International Union, United Automobile, Aerospace & Agricultural Implement Workers of America v. Dole*, 869 F.2d 616 (D.C. Cir. 1989).

[10] One of the boxes to check on the proposed LM-10 and 20 is "developing personnel policies or practices."

or indirect, of the persons activity …"[11] and "a consultant's revision of the employer's material or communications to enhance the persuasive message also triggers the duty to report …"[12] Even holding multi-employer "seminars, webinars and conferences that have as their "direct or indirect object to persuade employers concerning their representation or collective bargaining rights," would trigger a consultants or employers obligation to file the necessary reports.[13]

Under the proposed rule, the statutory section 203(c) exception would become so narrow as to be unrecognizable and, as discussed below, irrelevant. It would become a dead letter. The advice exception is narrowed by redefining "advice" extraordinarily narrowly. "A lawyer or other consultant, who exclusively counsels employer representatives on what they may lawfully say to employees, ensures a client's compliance with the law or provides guidance on NLRB practice or precedent is providing 'advice.'"[14] Period.

The Proposed Rule is Contrary to Congressional Intent

Notwithstanding the many unsubstantiated assertions in the proposed rule discussion that the proposed rule is designed to better reflect Congressional intent, there are at least five strong reasons to believe that the current rule reflects Congressional intent better than the proposed rule.

First, the 1959 Conference Committee Report explicitly stated that Congress intended the section 203(c) advice exception to be broad. It is, quite literally, difficult to conceive of a more narrowly drafted definition of advice than that contained in the proposed rule. Second, Congress has had five decades to change the code if it was dissatisfied with the Kennedy Administration interpretation. They have not. In fact, no corporate action of any kind has been taken by Congress. Neither chamber of Congress nor any committee of Congress has taken action to change the rule. This half century of Congressional acquiescence to the current interpretation is strong evidence that the Kennedy Administration DOL got it right (and every subsequent Administration for that matter). Third, the courts have found the current DOL rule to be consistent with Congressional intent. Fourth, basic rules of statutory construction would lead us to a different understanding of Congressional intent than that proffered by the authors of the proposed rule. The plain meaning of the word advice, whether used by a layman or an attorney, is much broader than the definition the authors of the proposed rule have chosen. No objective analyst could conclude that Congress meant so narrow an exception when it used the word advice. Fifth, the proposed rule's construction of the section 203(c) exception would make it quite literally a dead letter because under the proposed rule's exception language nothing would be exempt under section 203(c) that is not already exempt under section 204 (relating to attorney-client communications). It is inconsistent with basic rules of statutory construction to read a section of the statute as surplusage (i.e. unnecessary, unneeded or meaningless words) when an alternative construction gives meaning to the provision.

---

[11] *Federal Register*, Vol. 76, No. 119, June 21, 2011 at page 36191 (column 1).
[12] *Ibid.*
[13] *Federal Register*, Vol. 76, No. 119, June 21, 2011 at page 36191 (column 2).
[14] *Federal Register*, Vol. 76, No. 119, June 21, 2011 at page 36191 (column 1).

Congress Intended for the Exception to be Broad

Contrary to the assertion made in section IV (C) of the discussion in the proposed rule,[15] the 1959 Conference Committee report language makes the Congressional intent to grant a **broad** exemption patently clear. The proposed rule's discussion of Congressional intent is simply an attempt to obfuscate the issue.[16] The Conference Committee Report language with respect to the advice exception is set forth below.

Section 203-reports of employers

...

Subsection (c) of section 203 of the conference substitute grants a **broad** *(emphasis added)* exemption from the requirements of the section with respect to the giving of advice. This subsection is further discussed in connection with section 204.[17]

...

Section 204-attorney-client communications exempted

The senate bill provides that an attorney need not include in any report required by the act any information which was lawfully communicated to such attorney by any of his clients in the course of a legitimate attorney-client relationship.

The conference substitute adopts the provisions of the senate bill, but in connection therewith the conferees included, in section 203(c), a provision taken from the senate bill that provides that an employer or other person is not required to file a report covering the services of such person by reason of his giving or agreeing to give advice to such employer or representing or agreeing to represent such employer before any court, administrative agency, or tribunal of arbitration or engaging or agreeing to engage in collective bargaining on behalf of such employer or the negotiation of an agreement or any question arising thereunder.

---

[15] *Federal Register*, Vol. 76, No. 119, June 21, 2011 at page 36184.

[16] Quite literally none of the discussion in section IV(C) is relevant to the scope of the advice exception. The only part of the legislative history on point is reproduced here and makes it abundantly clear that the exception is to be broad rather than as narrow as it could conceivably be. The proposed regulation's authors seem to think that a discussion of the why the overall Act is necessary somehow trumps the only discussion of the advice exception. Again, elementary rules of construction and common sense dictate a more reasonable construction -- the construction that every DOL since the Kennedy Administration has adopted.

[17] Conf. Rep. 86-1147, Conf. Rep. No. 1147, 86TH Cong., 1st Sess. 1959, 1959 U.S.C.C.A.N. 2318, P.L. 86-257, Labor-Management Reporting and Disclosure Act of 1959.

Congress Has Knowingly Acquiesced to the Kennedy DOL Interpretation for Half a Century

The proposed rule seeks to change a rule in effect for half a century under Democratic and Republican Presidents and unchanged by Congress whether controlled by Democrats, Republicans or jointly. The fact that Congress has neither seen fit to change the underlying statute nor sought to invalidate the rule in any way for half a century is very strong evidence that Congress is satisfied with the current rule. In the last five decades, Congress has not passed legislation in either chamber changing this requirement nor has any committee reported out legislation making such a change. Nor, to our knowledge, has Congress even so much as held a hearing regarding the subject matter of the proposed rule (although the rule has been mentioned a few times by witnesses). This acquiescence by Congress belies the argument made in preamble to the proposed rule that the proposed changes are necessary to reflect the intention of Congress. We believe that Congress is satisfied with the current state of the law for the simple reason that there is no real problem with the law as it currently stands.

This argument is not only in accord with common sense but has long been recognized by the courts. See, e.g., *United States v. Midwest Oil Co.*, 236 U.S. 459 (1915). See also, *Kaplan v. Corcoran*, 545 F.2d 1073, (7th Cir. 1976).

The Courts Have Confirmed the Existing DOL Interpretation

Courts have upheld the current DOL interpretation of Congressional intent. For example, in the 1989 case, *International Union, United Automobile, Aerospace & Agricultural Implement Workers of America v. Dole*, [18] the Union appellees argued a position virtually identical to the position taken by the authors of the proposed rule. The D.C. Circuit Court disagreed.

The Circuit Court's discussion is directly on point and a good discussion of the current state of law:

> The Secretary reconciles section 203's coverage and exemption prescriptions differently. If the arrangement is one solely for advice to the employer and his supervisor representatives, then it matters not, according to the Secretary, that the advice has as "an object" employee persuasion. The very purpose of section 203's exemption prescription, the Secretary maintains, is to remove from the section's coverage certain activity that otherwise would have been reportable. In the overlap area, the Secretary thus concludes, the exemption direction, not the coverage provision, generally must control.

> Given the tension Congress created, and the deference due the Secretary's reconciliation, we cannot call arbitrary her view that if an activity is properly characterized as "advice," reporting generally is not required. We therefore proceed to inquire whether the Secretary has reasonably delineated what constitutes advice within the meaning of section 203(c), 29 U.S.C. Sec. 433(c).

---

[18] 869 F.2d 616 (D.C. Cir. 1989).

The statute itself, always the starting point, nowhere attempts a definition of the term. See Memorandum from Charles Donahue, Solicitor of Labor, to John L. Holcombe, Commissioner, Bureau of Labor-Management Reports, at 1 (Feb. 19, 1962).

In a 1962 effort to describe the "advice" exemption, LMRDA Interpretative Manual Entry Sec. 265.005 (Jan. 19, 1962) (Scope of the "Advice" Exemption), the Department contrasted 1) material a consultant delivers directly to employees to persuade them regarding organizational rights, with 2) material the employer drafts, then refers to a consultant for review or revision. The first category falls outside, and the second, inside, the advice exemption. There is no dispute over either of these rankings.

The "more difficult" to classify cases, the Department has acknowledged, involve presentations for and to the employer prepared entirely by the consultant, e.g., a fully scripted speech for supervisors to deliver. In such cases, it has been the Department's policy that where the employer is free to accept or reject the written material prepared for him and there is no indication that the middleman is operating under a deceptive arrangement with the employer, the fact that the middleman drafts the material in its entirety will not in itself generally be sufficient to require a report.

...

Recognizing the Secretary's right to shape her enforcement policy to the realities of limited resources and competing priorities, and comprehending her ruling on advice to involve no *volte face* from longstanding statutory definition and interpretation, we reject the challenge to her ruling.

No court has held that an attorney or consultant that provides only advice and has no contact with employees must file reports.

There is No Reason to Part from the Ordinary Meaning of the Word Advice

There is absolutely no reason to believe that those drafting the Act meant something unusual when they used the word advice in the statute. There is certainly no reason to believe that they meant to exclude most categories of advice when they used the word advice. Had they meant to exclude only lawyers in administrative proceedings or providing the narrowest kind of legal advice, they would have said so.[19] They undoubtedly intended what they said and Congress in enacting the legislation did not assume some oddly narrow definition of the word. That they did not define the word in the statute strongly implies they used the word in its ordinary sense. In accordance with the canons of statutory construction, in the absence of any clear evidence to the contrary and explicit legislative history saying they meant for the advice exception to be broad, the word advice should be construed in accordance with its ordinary meaning. The Supreme

---

[19] And section 203(c) would be unnecessary in light of section 204 (regarding attorney-client privilege), as discussed below.

Court has held that "statutory words are presumed, unless the contrary appears, to be used in their ordinary sense, with the meaning commonly attributed to them."[20] The proposed rule, if finalized, would constitute an abuse of discretion by the DOL because it construes the word advice in an abusively narrow manner. The proposed rule does not further Congressional intent. Instead, it is in direct contravention of clearly expressed Congressional intent.

The Proposed Rule Effectively Reads Section 203(c) Out of the Law

The proposed rule's construction of the section 203(c) exception would make it quite literally a dead letter because under the proposed rule's exception language nothing would be exempt under the new interpretation of section 203(c) that is not already exempt under section 204 (relating to attorney-client communications). It is inconsistent with basic rules of statutory construction to read a section of the statute as surplusage (i.e. unnecessary, unneeded or meaningless words) when an alternative construction gives meaning to the provision.

The Supreme Court has held that "[i]t is the duty of the Court to give effect, if possible, to every clause and word of a statute, avoiding, if it may be, any construction which implies that the legislature was ignorant of the meaning of the language it employed."[21]

Section 204 provides:

Sec. 204. Nothing contained in this Act shall be construed to require an attorney who is a member in good standing of the bar of any State, to include in any report required to be filed pursuant to the provisions of this Act any information which was lawfully communicated to such attorney by any of his clients in the course of a legitimate attorney-client relationship.

The proposed rule would limit the advice exception by defining advice as follows:

A lawyer or other consultant, who exclusively counsels employer representatives on what they may lawfully say to employees, ensures a client's compliance with the law or provides guidance on NLRB practice or precedent is providing "advice."[22]

There is virtually no advice that meets the proposed definition of advice that would not also be protected by section 204. Ergo, the proposed rule quite literally reads section 203(c) out of the law and violates the canons of statutory construction laid down by the Supreme Court.

The Proposed Rule Upends a Half Century of Settled Law, Creates Uncertainty and Replaces a Clear Bright Line Rule with One Riddled with Ambiguity

While it is clear that the authors of the proposed rule want to broaden LMRDA dramatically, it is not clear where they really mean for the line to be drawn. After half of century of practice,

---

[20] *Caminetti v. United States*, 242 U.S. 470, 471 (1917).
[21] *Montclair v. Ramsdell*, 107 U.S. 147, 152 (1883).
[22] Federal Register, Vol. 76, No. 119, June 21, 2011 at page 36191 (column 1).

guidance and court rulings, the scope of the current rule is well known. Replacing the current rule will create uncertainty, require firms to spend time and money evaluating the new rule and consulting with their attorneys and other advisors. And, notwithstanding all of that effort, it will be years before the final contours of the new rule are known.

These costs are generally underappreciated by government regulators in any event. But at this time of economic difficulty, imposing additional costs and creating additional uncertainty is particularly ill-advised.

NSBA is gravely concerned by the implication in the proposed regulation that modifications of personnel policies and practices fall under the persuader activities list. This concern is further bolstered by the fact one of the boxes to check on the proposed LM-10 and 20 is "developing personnel policies or practices." Any prudent business has its employee handbook reviewed for reasons entirely unrelated to union organizing or labor disputes. Yet, under the proposed rule, this could be construed to be persuader activity and apply to the attorneys, insurance agents, HR consultants, pension consultants, accountants or financial advisors who review benefits packages or other personnel practices. Given the civil and criminal penalties associated with the Act, such a broad reporting requirement is totally unwarranted and deeply troubling.

A final point. The proposed rule provides that even multiemployer "seminars, webinars and conferences that have as their "direct or indirect object to persuade employers concerning their representation or collective bargaining rights," would trigger an obligation by "the consultant and the employer … to file the necessary reports."[23] A law firm, consulting firm, trade association, professional association or other entity that puts on a seminar, webinar or conference regarding the advice exception or other labor law issues typically has no idea what those hearing the presentation are going to do with the information. Absent mind reading skills, it will be impossible for them to comply with the rule unless they report all attendees to their events and the fees that they paid. This constitutes a grave violation of privacy and a tremendous administrative burden on providers. It will reduce the number of informational programs and will increase their cost. It will lead to a less informed business and inevitably result in less, not more, compliance with the law.

The Proposed Rule Imposes Substantially Higher Costs than the DOL claims

The DOL analysis of the cost of the proposed rule does a better job than most of providing the logic and basis of its cost analysis. For this, the agency is to be commended. However, the analysis is substantially flawed and potentially under estimates the cost that the proposed rule would impose by an order of magnitude or, probably, more. In short, the estimate is very, very wrong.

First, the reporting obligations imposed by the new rule are extremely broad. Reporting obligations fall on anyone who may indirectly or direct be involved in persuasion. This goes far beyond the 3,414 Form LM-10 filers and the 2,601 Form LM-20 filers that the Department estimates. If the proposed rule is to be taken seriously (and because of the associated criminal penalties for non-filing, it must be), virtually every lawyer, consultant, advisor, publisher, web

---

[23] *Federal Register*, Vol. 76, No. 119, June 21, 2011 at page 36191 (column 2).

page consultant and the like who works for a firm with a labor union that may have a labor dispute will end up having to familiarize themselves with these rules and may well have to file.

Thus instead of 6,000 filers, the DOL may see ten times that many or more.

Second, the time estimates (60 minutes for an LM-20 and 120 minutes for an LM-10) are dramatically too low.[24] Perhaps, a labor lawyer already familiar with the rule and the underlying law who also had taken an Evelyn Wood speed reading course and had highly efficient support staff could meet these times if only one consultant is involved. Perhaps. But most business people are going to have to spend time familiarizing themselves with the LMRDA, the rules promulgated thereunder and any DOL issued guidance, then go on to familiarize themselves with the forms, then collect the information necessary and then fill out the form. Moreover, given the breadth of the proposed rule, employers are likely to have many, not just one, consultant that is reportable.

Third, given the complexity and ambiguity of the law and the potential criminal penalties involved, any prudent affected employer is going to seek outside advice regarding compliance from an attorney or consultant expert. This will take time and cost a considerable amount of money. Yet the DOL cost estimates do not take into account the cost of outside advice.

We suggest the following empirical experiment. Give random persons a copy of the law and the regulations and copies of DOL guidance. Then give them a reasonable fact pattern. Then tell them to figure out whether they need to file and, if so, to prepare the forms correctly. Then tell them they will go to prison if they are wrong. We suggest that they will not be able to complete this task in 60 to 120 minutes. And that they probably would want to consult an expert before filing the forms. Of course, a more realistic experiment would entail them having to find the law, the regulations and the guidance on their own. The idea that firms are going to be able to comply with this rule for $87 to $175 is simply ludicrous.[25]

The Proposed Rule will Harm Employers' Right to Secure Advice

By imposing such a burden on employers securing advice, the proposed rule would act as a substantial deterrent to employers securing advice. This effect is likely to be particularly pronounced on small employers that have limited funds, cannot afford expensive advice and do not have in-house counsel. This is undoubtedly part of the unstated agenda of supporters of the rule. An unintended consequence of the proposed rule is that by dramatically increasing the cost and consequences (potential criminal penalties) of securing advice, fewer firms will seek advice and compliance with important aspects of the National Labor Relations Act will decline.

---

[24] *Federal Register*, Vol. 76, No. 119, June 21, 2011 at pages 36198-36204.
[25] *Federal Register*, Vol. 76, No. 119, June 21, 2011 at page 36203.

The Proposed Rule Violates Attorney-Client Privilege

The authors of the proposed rule wrongly assert that "In general, the fact of legal consultation, clients' identities, attorney's fees and the scope and nature of the employment are not deemed privileged."[26]

The American Bar Association Model Rules of Professional Conduct have been adopted, with modifications, in most states. Rule 1.6 of the Model Rules has routinely been interpreted to prohibit attorneys from disclosing, without client consent, the existence of an attorney-client relationship and the fee arrangement. It also, of course, protects attorney client communication. Merely by providing a client with advice beyond the narrow confines of the exception set forth in the Proposed Rule, the Proposed Form LM-10 not only would require the disclosure of an attorney-client relationship, the size of the fee and the full contents of the engagement agreement, part C of the form would also require that the attorneys' activities be disclosed with specificity. The Proposed Rule would, therefore, force attorneys either to violate the disciplinary rules that govern their practice of law and face disbarment or to violate the regulations implementing the LMRDA and face criminal sanctions under that Act. Thus, the Proposed Rule places attorneys in a manifestly absurd position. This situation will engender great uncertainty and adversely affect the trust between attorney and client. It will harm their ability to provide sound advice and the ability of their employer clients to obtain sound advice.

Moreover, section 204 of the LMRDA makes it clear that the proposed rule is blatantly inconsistent with the underlying statute. Section 204 provides:

Attorney-Client Communications Exempted

> Sec. 204. Nothing contained in this Act shall be construed to require an attorney who is a member in good standing of the bar of any State, to include in any report required to be filed pursuant to the provisions of this Act any information which was lawfully communicated to such attorney by any of his clients in the course of a legitimate attorney-client relationship.[27]

The proposed rule should be withdrawn both because it is inconsistent with the clear Congressional intent to protect attorney-client privilege expressed by section 204 and because it is inconsistent with the attorney disciplinary rules in most if not all U.S. jurisdictions.

The Proposed Rule Lacks an Adequate Evidentiary Basis

It is unclear to the NSBA how dramatically increasing reporting and increasing business compliance costs is going to have a meaningful positive impact on working Americans. Nor does the NSBA membership believe that there is a meaningful problem that this proposed regulation is addressing. Yes, there are consultants that provide advice to employers. Generally, they help firms navigate the thicket of labor laws that a firm must comply with. They also, of

---

[26] *Federal Register*, Vol. 76, No. 119, June 21, 2011 at page 36192 (column 1).
[27] 29 USC 434.

course, may assist a firm in achieving a desired result in a labor dispute or prevailing in an NLRB election. We see nothing inherently wrong with that. It is not as if labor unions do not engage consultants.

If consultants or lawyers are engaging in unlawful practices, then the DOL should use the many tools available to it to attack that problem rather than imposing an additional compliance burden on the small business community. But radically increasing reporting is not going to materially improve DOL's ability to police unlawful practices since neither employers nor consultants engaging in such practices are going to report doing so.

Accelerated Union Elections

In June, 2011, the NLRB published a proposed rule that would revise election procedures so that in most cases elections would be conducted 10 to 21 days after the filing of the petition.[28] Currently, most elections are conducted 35 to 40 days after filing of the petition and cannot be conducted before 25 days have elapsed. The rule accomplishes this acceleration by limiting pre and post election hearings and appeals primarily relating to bargaining unit scope, and voter eligibility issues. The rule is sometimes referred to as the "quickie election rule" or the "ambush election rule."

In December, a revised and final rule was published[29] and it took effect in April, 2012. On May 14, 2012, the U.S. District Court for the District of Columbia granted summary judgment to employer groups challenging the rule on the procedural grounds that the NLRB did not have a quorum when it adopted the rule.[30] The court did not address the substantive objections raised in the lawsuit.[31] NLRB then suspended implementation of the new rule.

With the confirmation of five members of the NLRB and the consequent end of the lack of a quorum issue, there is every reason to believe that the Board will revisit the accelerated election rule.

The reasons that the NLRB majority gave in support of the changes were "to remove the most obviously unnecessary steps in the representation-case process" and to "eliminate unnecessary litigation." These are laudable goals that NSBA shares. Litigation costs can be a crushing burden for small employers and there is little doubt that the current process can be streamlined. However, we believe that the proposed rule has two basic infirmities. First, it effectively denies due process to employers and, second, it makes the election process fundamentally unfair.[32]

Our biggest concern is that the rule so accelerates representation elections that few employers and almost no small employers will be able to fairly and fully present their views to employees.

---

[28] "Representation—Case Procedures," *Federal Register*, Vol. 76, No. 120, June 22, 2011, p. 36812.
[29] "Representation—Case Procedures," *Federal Register*, Vol. 76, No. 246, December 22, 2011, p. 80138.
[30] *Chamber of Commerce v. NLRB*, May 14, 2012 (DCDC), Civil Action No. 11-2262 (opinion of James E. Boasberg).
[31] The substantive challenges being that the rule violates the First and Fifth Amendments and that the rule exceeds the NLRB's statutory authority.
[32] It is not clear whether the rule sufficiently deprive litigants of due process so as to run afoul of constitutional guarantees.

Therefore, both employers and employees will be ill served because there will not be a complete airing of the issues involved and employees will be forced to vote with incomplete information.

NLRB Chairman Pearce in a Separate Concurring Statement wrote:

> However long the time from petition to election, it is the same for both parties. The Board's analysis does not play favorites between the parties. As the rule explains, if 10 days has always been enough for the union to campaign with the Excelsior list, then even 10 days from the petition would be enough for the employer (who needs no such list of employees) to campaign, too.[33]

This is deeply disingenuous.

The members of this committee know a thing or two about elections. I invite each member of this committee to undertake a thought experiment.

Imagine if your opponent was permitted to organize his or her campaign, raise money, hire consultants, recruit volunteers, communicate with voters and only then were you informed that there was an election coming up and it would be in 10 days. Perhaps I am wrong, but I doubt anyone in this hearing room would regard this as fair in the context of elections for public office. It is, I submit, no more fair in elections determining whether or not a union will collectively bargain for employees

Unions will have spent months organizing and laying the groundwork before filing an election petition. Unions know labor law and have counsel with expertise. Unions are experts at waging unionization campaigns. Most small employees, in contrast, do not know anything about the law relating to representation elections, and do not have attorneys on staff. Under the proposed rules, they will be accorded only 10 days to find counsel, inform them of the facts, develop their message and campaign materials and communicate to employees.

The Supreme Court has on many occasions noted that Congress intended for the election process to be robust, most recently in the 2008 case *Chamber of Commerce v. Brown*.[34] In that decision, the court noted:

> We have characterized this policy judgment which suffuses the NLRA as a whole as favoring uninhibited, robust and wide open debate in labor disputes, stressing that freewheeling use of the written and spoken word ... has been expressly fostered by Congress and approved by the NLRB.[35]

A review of the legislative history makes it clear that this analysis is correct.[36]

---

[33] *Federal Register*, Vol. 77, No. 83, April 30, 2012, p. 25558.

[34] 554 U.S. 60, 128 S. Ct. 2408 (2008).

[35] *Brown*, quoting *Letter Carriers v. Austin*, 418 U.S. 264, 272-273 (1974).

[36] See Joseph P. Mastrosimone, "Limiting Information in the Information Age: The NLRB's Misguided Attempt to Squelch Employer Speech," 52 Washburn Law Journal 473 (2013), especially pp. 486-493. The amendments to the NLRA (1935, the "Wagner Act," P.L. 74-198) made by the Labor Management Relations Act of 1947 (the Taft–Hartley Act, P.L. 80–101) are the foundation of modern labor law. Taft–Hartley created statutory protections for employer

In the event that the NLRB goes down this path again, we support the *Workforce Democracy and Fairness Act*,[37] particularly the provision which provides that no NLRB election will be held in less than 35 days after filing of the petition.

Micro Unions

In *Specialty Healthcare*[38] the NLRB started the process of dismantling the traditionally understood "community of interest" rule for determining bargaining units. The NLRB allowed the initial bargaining unit to be a single job description, namely certified nursing assistants. In *Specialty Healthcare*, the NLRB enunciated a new standard that in effects allows unions to determine the bargaining unit (i..e. the representation election electorate) and the union determination is presumed correct unless the employer "demonstrates that employees in the larger unit share an overwhelming community of interest with those in the petitioned-for unit." As discussed below, this presumption that the union determination of bargaining unit is correct appears to be virtually irrebuttable.

Employers expressed concern at the time that the *Specialty Healthcare* decision would result in a proliferation of bargaining units and allow unions to balkanize the workplace, forcing employers to deal with a potentially huge number of unions. In addition, it appeared to allow unions to organize very small parts of a company's workforce, even if the overwhelming majority of employees opposed unionization, by picking occupations or departments where they believed they could achieve a majority. Thus, they would be able to partially organize employers where they would have no chance of prevailing under traditional rules.

Within months, these concerns proved more than justified.

For example, in *Northrop Grumman*[39] the union was permitted to organize a departmental unit of 223 radiological control and other technicians out of 2400 technical employees and 18,500 Northrop employees overall at the shipyard.

The most egregious example I know of is the *Bergdorf Goodman*[40] case. The union sought to represent all full-time and regular part-time women's shoes associates in the 2nd Floor Designer Shoes Department and in the 5th Floor Contemporary Shoes Department. The employer asserted that the smallest appropriate unit must be comprised of a store-wide unit, or in the alternative, all

---

speech and employer involvement in the elections process. Sen. Taft: "… the bill contains a provision guaranteeing free speech to employers." Rep. Hartley: "One of the main purposes of the Act was to guarantee "employees and employers, and their respective representatives, the full exercise of free speech." See *Southern Colorado Power Co.*, 13 NLRB 699 (1939) for a discussion of pre Taft-Hartley law ("almost any expression of opinion by an employer expressing disapproval of a labor organization is unlawful"); see also "Paul L. Herzog and Howard A. Rikoon, "The Employer and the First Amendment," St. John's Law Review, Vol. 22, No. 1, November 1947.

[37] H.R. 3094, 112th Congress.

[38] *Specialty Healthcare and Rehabilitation Center of Mobile*, NLRB (December 22, 2010 and August 26, 2011).

[39] *Northrop Grumman Shipbuilding, Inc. and International Association Of Machinists And Aerospace Workers, AFL–CIO*, NLRB (December 30, 2011).

[40] The Neiman Marcus Group, Inc., D/B/A Bergdorf Goodman v. Local 1102 Retail, Wholesale Department Store Union, NLRB (May 4, 2012).

selling associates in the store. The NLRB allowed the union chosen bargaining unit of 46 employees in the 2nd and 5th floor shoe departments to be separately organized.

The *Specialty Healthcare, Northrop Grumman* and *Bergdorf Goodman* cases represent a path that is not warranted by the underlying law[41] and is a stark departure from decades of NLRB practice. It certainly is good for labor attorneys given the complexity, litigation and proliferation of bargaining units it will engender. It may prove to be good for unions because they will be able to unionize small groups of employees in workplaces they would not otherwise be able to unionize.

It is undoubtedly bad for employers because of the huge increase in costs it will cause and the substantially complexity and reduced flexibility caused by a proliferation in the number of bargaining units. There is absolutely no reason to believe that increasing the costs to employers and complexity in the workplace will do anything material to help employees.

It is our hope, if not our expectation, that the NLRB will walk back from this line of cases. If not, then we would expect the courts to require the adoption of more reasonable bargaining unit rules more in keeping with the NLRA. If they do not, however, we would urge Congress to step in and adopt legislation providing for clear and reasonable rules governing the size and number of bargaining units at a workplace.

NLRB Social Media Policies

Section 7 of the National Labor Relations Act reads:

> **Employees shall have the right** to self-organization, to form, join, or assist labor organizations, to bargain collectively through representatives of their own choosing, and **to engage in other concerted activities for the purpose of collective bargaining or other mutual aid or protection,** and shall also have the right to refrain from any or all of such activities except to the extent that such right may be affected by an agreement requiring membership in a labor organization as a condition of employment as authorized in section 8(a)(3). (emphasis added)[42]

This protection of "concerted activities" applies to all employees working for employers subject to the jurisdiction of the NLRB. This includes a huge swath of the non-unionized workforce. In June, 2012, the NLRB launched a web site directed at providing information regarding protected concerted activity and seeking complainants. See www.nlrb.gov/concerted-activity.

As part of its general initiative regarding protected concerted activities, NLRB General Counsel's office has issued a series of three Operations-Management memoranda regarding how the NLRB believes that employers' rules governing the use of social media might contravene employees' section 7 rights.[43] Operations-Management memoranda are issued to the field

[41] Namely section 9 of the NLRA.
[42] 29 USC 157.
[43] August 18, 2011 (OM 11-74), January 24, 2012 (OM 12-31), and May 30, 2012 (OM 12-59)

offices from the Division of Operations-Management of the General Counsel's Office to give direction to regional offices in case handling matters.

Before addressing our serious concerns with NLRB policies in this area, I would like to commend the agency in one important respect. In the most recent Operations-Management memorandum (May 30, 2012), the NLRB provided a model Social Media Policy that it finds acceptable. Entirely independent of the merits of the model policy, this is a very constructive step because small business owners, their attorneys and their advocates can read it and know what NLRB finds acceptable. The NLRB approach contrasts favorably, for example, with the EEOC approach on criminal background screening. The EEOC has issued a 55 page, 167 footnote "guidance" document which provides no meaningful guidance as to what is and is not acceptable in their view regarding the use of conviction records.[44]

That said, there are aspects of the current NLRB approach to social media that are very difficult to understand. For example, the NLRB deems unlawful the seemingly common sense instruction that "[o]ffensive, demeaning, abusive or inappropriate remarks are as out of place online as they are offline."[45] NLRB argues that "this provision proscribes a broad spectrum of communications that would include protected criticisms of the employer's labor policies or treatment of employees." It is, to be charitable, doubtful that section 7 protects "offensive, demeaning, abusive or inappropriate remarks." It is, in contrast, quite likely that employers that permit the use of such language would find themselves liable under other theories (sexual harassment, civil rights violations, etc.). I would like to think that federal law is not that the employer is liable whether they prohibit inappropriate speech or permit it.[46]

The core point of the employer's handbook language rejected by the NLRB above is, I believe, accurate. The section 7 analysis should not vary depending on how the speech was made. If it is inappropriate in one medium, then it is inappropriate in another. Conversely, speech that is protected is protected whether it is made in person, on-line, over the telephone or by some other mechanism. It is a mistake for the NLRB to treat speech differently depending on how it is transmitted rather than what it says or to whom it was directed.

The September 28, 2012 NLRB decision in *Knauz BMW* is based on a similar "analysis" and is particularly remarkable. It shows how unmoored from the underlying purpose or language of section 7 the NLRB has become in the social media area. The employer's employee handbook contained the following language which was deemed a violation of the employees' rights:

> Courtesy is the responsibility of every employee. Everyone is expected to be courteous, polite and friendly to our customers, vendors and suppliers, as well as to their fellow employees. No one should be disrespectful or use profanity or any other language which injures the image or reputation of the Dealership.

---

[44] The "guidance" does make two things clear: The use of arrest records (as opposed to conviction records) is ill advised and the mere fact that a state or local law requires a business to bar certain felons from certain jobs will not protect the business owner from EEOC enforcement action. Other than that, I would recommend the guidance to law school professors as an example of how **not** to conduct legal writing.

[45] OM 12-59, May 30, 2012.

[46] I hesitate entirely ruling out the possibility. See note 44 above regarding the EEOC.

Thus, the NLRB has now ruled that requiring courtesy is unlawful. According to the NLRB, "Employees would reasonably construe its broad prohibition against disrespectful conduct and language which injures the image or reputation of the Dealership as encompassing Section 7 activity." I find it utterly implausible that the authors of section 7 intended to prevent employers from requiring employees to be courteous to their customers or fellow employers. It is a mystery why, as a matter of policy, we should want to encourage employees to be discourteous to each other or their employers' customers. I would hope that that the courts will find this beyond the scope of *Chevron* deference.

In its September 7, 2012 *Costco Wholesale Corporation* decision, the NLRB held that Costco's social media policy was unlawful. The board found that the policy—which prohibited Costco employees from making statements on social media that could damage the company or damage any person's reputation—could violate employees' free speech rights under section 7 of the NLRA. This decision, while questionable, is at least plausibly related to the purposes of the NLRA in that Costco's policy, which was quite broad ("damage the company" or "damage any person's reputation"), could be read as limiting protected speech.

Conclusion

Both the DOL and the NLRB are taking actions, or are likely to take actions, inconsistent with the laws enacted by Congress. These actions will also impose a tremendous burden on small firms and are fundamentally unfair. They will harm job creation and create needless costs. We have asked the agencies to rethink these actions. If they do not, it is our hope that the courts will correct the agencies' excesses. If they do not, we would urge Congress to do so.

Chairman ROE. Thank you, Mr. Burton.
Mr. Adams?

STATEMENT OF MR. CLARENCE ADAMS, FIELD TECHNICIAN, CABLEVISION, BROOKLYN, NY

Mr. ADAMS. Thank you. Thank you, Mr. Chairman, Ranking Member Andrews, and members of the subcommittee for giving me this opportunity to testify. I appreciate it greatly. Thank you very much.

My name is Clarence Adams, and I have been a field technician for Cablevision in Brooklyn for over 14 years. I am also a proud veteran of the United States Marines. And 10 years ago, I was among the first wave of American troops who invaded Iraq. I was proud to serve my country and was prepared to do whatever was necessary to define the basic freedoms that make this country great.

I want to tell you today that my coworkers and I have gone through a lot to try to join a union. In the fall of—I am sorry, in the winter of 2011 myself and a large group of coworkers decided to organize with the Communication Workers of America. Company management viciously opposed our efforts. I was forced to attend literally dozens of meetings where Cablevision management told me that CWA was corrupt. They lied to me about the cost of dues and the likelihood of strikes. They threatened that my wages and benefits would actually go down if we joined together in a union.

But on January 26, 2012 an overwhelming majority of my coworkers in Brooklyn voted to join CWA. We were very excited. We thought now we would be able to sit down with Cablevision and negotiate a contract that reasonably addresses our concerns. But we were wrong. I soon learned that management had no intention of bargaining with us in good faith. They continued their campaign of pressure and intimidation. And as a union supporter, I felt like I was under the microscope every day when I went to work.

A few months after we won our election, my Cablevision workers in the Bronx and I decided—my Cablevision workers in Bronxville decided to begin organizing as well and join CWA. In late April, James Dolan, the CEO of Cablevision, made it clear that he would stop at nothing to prevent more employees from joining our union. Dolan gave every single employee in the entire company, about $10,000, significant raises, except for us in Brooklyn. He improved the health plans of every single employee in Cablevision except for us in Brooklyn.

He allowed techs all over his company to install Wi-Fi in parks, except for us in Brooklyn. The only difference between those of us in Brooklyn and the rest of the company was that we exercised our legal rights to join a union. Right before my coworkers in the Bronx held a vote on joining the union in late June, James Dolan personally visited them and stated that they shouldn't make the same mistake we did in Brooklyn. He told them that Cablevision would now abandon Brooklyn. He told them Brooklyn would be left behind in terms of investment in workforce.

Management succeeded in frightening enough workers so that a majority voted against the union. Earlier this year, on January 30, I was among 70 Cablevision workers in Brooklyn who decided to take advantage of the company's open door policy, which encourages employees to go to management at any time to discuss issues of concern. I arrived, before my shift started, to meet with a manager, any manager, for only 5 minutes to express my frustration that the company was stalling during bargaining.

That morning, management eventually agreed to invite 22 techs into a conference room, and I was one of those techs. I was shocked to find that vice president, Mr. Rick Levesque, came into the room and told us we were all being permanently replaced. Cablevision's open door policy specifically says that the company does not tolerate retaliation against employees for having views different from their own, but on this day that policy wasn't worth the paper it was written on.

Thanks to a massive pressure campaign, the company has been forced to hire all of us back. I am proud to say that my 21 coworkers and I, who were fired, stayed strong through the entire ordeal. And when we walked back in the door, we showed our fellow coworkers that this is a fight that we can still win. But I have to say that I am very, very upset about what happened to us and what has happened since we voted the union in.

The NLRB had filed charges against Cablevision, and we still await justice. Cablevision threatened my livelihood by illegally firing me, and they have shown utter contempt for the rule of the law. And so far, there have been no consequences for them. Cablevision has hired over 50 lawyers, literally, to defend their unlawful actions. It is simply obscene for them to spend so much on lawyers instead of sitting down to negotiate with their employees.

I just want a shot at the American dream. I want job security. I want to know that I can't be fired without just cause. Ten years ago, I put my life on the line 6,000 miles away from home in the name of protecting the basic rights of American democracy. I believe I was fighting so that the rights of every American would be protected. I never thought that I would see the day that I, as an American citizen, would have my basic rights trampled on, and no one would do anything about it.

I never thought that a big corporation could violate my rights, and the government would just let them get away with it. I am sad to say that my experience has taught me that our current labor laws are broken. Workers who dream of reaching the middle class and who hope for some job security shouldn't have to endure months, or even years, of fear and intimidation at work. I was there when my country asked me to risk everything in Iraq, and is it too much to ask for my government to protect my rights to join a union at work?

Thank you for giving me the opportunity to share my story with you today. Thank you.

[The statement of Mr. Adams follows:]

Testimony of

Clarence Adams

Before the Subcommittee on

Health, Employment, Labor and Pensions

Hearing on

"The Future of Union Organizing"

September 19, 2013

Thank you Mr. Chairman, Ranking Member Andrews and members of this subcommittee for giving me the opportunity to testify.

My name is Clarence Adams and I have been a field technician for Cablevision in Brooklyn for over 14 years. I am also a proud veteran of the US Marines. Ten years ago, I was among the first wave of American troops who invaded Iraq. I was proud to serve my country and I was prepared to do whatever was necessary to defend the basic freedoms that make this a great country.

I want to tell you today what I and my coworkers have gone through just to try to join a union.

In the fall and winter of 2011, I and a large group of my co-workers decided to organize with the Communications Workers of America.

Company management viciously opposed our efforts. I was forced to attend literally dozens of meetings where Cablevision management told me CWA was corrupt. They lied to me about the cost of dues and the likelihood of strikes. They threatened that my wages and benefits would actually go down if we joined together into a union. But on January 26, 2012, an overwhelming majority of my coworkers in Brooklyn voted to join CWA.

We were so excited. We thought, now we'll sit down with Cablevision and negotiate a contract that reasonably addresses our concerns.

We were wrong. I soon learned that management had no intention of bargaining with us in good faith. They continued their campaign of pressure and intimidation. As a union supporter, I felt like I was under a microscope every day I went to work.

A few months after we won our election, my Cablevision coworkers in the Bronx decided to begin organizing as well, to join us in CWA.

In late April, James Dolan, the CEO of Cablevision, made it clear that he would stop at nothing to prevent more employees from joining our union. Dolan gave every single employee in the entire company - about 10,000 people - significant raises. Except for us in Brooklyn. He improved the health plans of every single employee in Cablevision. Except for us in Brooklyn. He allowed techs all over his company to install Wi-Fi in parks. Except for us in Brooklyn. The only difference between those of us in Brooklyn and the rest of the company was that we exercised our legal rights to join a union.

And then, right before my coworkers in the Bronx held a vote on joining the union in late June, James Dolan personally visited them and stated that they shouldn't make the same mistake we did in Brooklyn. He told them that Cablevision would now "abandon" Brooklyn. He told them Brooklyn would be left behind in terms of investment and the workforce. Management succeeded in frightening enough workers so that a majority voted against the union.

Early this year, on January 30th, I was among 70 Cablevision workers in Brooklyn who decided to take advantage of the company's "Open Door Policy", which encourages employees to go to management at anytime to discuss issues of concern.

I arrived before my shift started to meet with a manager, any manager, for only five minutes to express my frustration that the company was stalling during bargaining. That morning, management eventually agreed to invite 22 techs into a conference room. I was one of those techs.

I was shocked when the Vice President, Mr. Rick Levesque, came into the room and told us we were being "permanently replaced."

Cablevision's "Open Door Policy" specifically says that the company "does not tolerate retaliation against employees for having views different from ours," but on this day, that policy wasn't worth the paper it was written on.

Thanks to a massive pressure campaign, the company has been forced to hire all of us back. I am proud that my 21 co-workers and I who were fired stayed strong through this ordeal. And when we walked back in the door, we showed our fellow workers that this is still a fight that we can win.

But I have to say I am very, very upset about what happened to us and what has happened since we voted in the union. The NLRB has filed charges against Cablevision, and we still await justice. Cablevision threatened my livelihood by illegally firing me, and they have shown utter contempt for the rule of law. And so far there have been no consequences for them. Cablevision has hired over 50 lawyers, literally, to defend their unlawful actions. It is simply obscene for them to spend so much on lawyers, instead of sitting down to negotiate with their employees.

I just want a shot at the American Dream. I want some job security. I want to know that I can't be fired without just cause.

Ten years ago, I put my life on the line 6,000 miles away from home in the name of protecting the basic rights of American democracy. I believed I was fighting so that the rights of every American would be protected. I never thought that I would see the day that I, as an American citizen, would have my basic rights trampled on and no one would do anything about it. I never thought that a big corporation could violate my rights and the government would let them get away with it.

I am sad to say that my experience has taught me that our current labor laws are broken. Workers who dream of reaching the middle class and who hope for some job security shouldn't have to endure months and even years of fear and intimidation at work.

I was there when my country asked me to risk everything in Iraq. Is it too much to ask for my government to protect my right to join a union at work?

Thank you for giving me the opportunity to share my story with you today.

———

Chairman ROE. Thank you, Mr. Adams.
Mr. Marculewicz?

STATEMENT OF MR. STEFAN J. MARCULEWICZ, SHAREHOLDER, LITTLER MEMDELSON, WASHINGTON, DC

Mr. MARCULEWICZ. Chairman Roe, Ranking Member Andrews and the members of the committee, I want to thank you all for the opportunity to offer testimony this morning on this important topic. My name is Stefan Marculewicz. I am a shareholder with the law firm of Littler Mendelson here in Washington, D.C. I am speaking to you today on my own behalf and not on behalf of my firm or any firm client or anyone else.

I have practiced law, or labor employment law, for nearly 20 years. I started my career at the National Labor Relations Board in Forth Worth, Texas as a field attorney, and also worked for a time in Baltimore, Maryland at the regional office there, as well.

Labor unions, as Chairman Roe indicated, the primary advocate for workers' rights in the United States for more than a century, have experienced a significant decline in membership. As a result, labor unions have sought new and innovative means to effectuate change in the workplace. One of the most significant examples of this effort is the development of organizations known as worker centers. In recent months, these groups have been involved in protests and other activities that have received substantial coverage in the media.

Typically, they are non-profit organizations that receive funding from foundations, grants, including from government, membership fees and other donations. Some are funded by other labor organizations. These groups offer a variety of services to their members, including education, training, employment services and legal advice. Increasingly, however, worker centers are directly engaging employers or groups of employers to effectuate change in the wages, hours, and terms and conditions of employment of the workers they claim to represent.

Indeed, when it comes to such direct engagement, these worker centers often act no differently than traditional labor unions. Yet few of these groups comply with the laws that regulate labor organizations. Statutes, like the National Labor Relations Act and the Labor, Management, Reporting and Disclosure Act, contain significant protections with respect to representational democracy, organizational democracy, access to basic information and promotion of the duty of fair representation.

These basic rights are an important part of the process governing the representation of employees in the workplace by third-party organizations. Even though compliance with these laws would confer benefits upon the very workers these groups claim to represent, many such groups are reluctant to define themselves as labor organizations because the NLRA and LMRDA are perceived as creating an impediment to worker centers' activities. In addition, worker centers have not considered themselves to be limited by the NLRA restrictions on secondary picketing and protracted picketing for recognition.

And such conduct is a common tool used by these groups to convey their message, although it would violate the National Labor Relations Act. Without coverage of the NLRA and LMRDA, these organizations can avoid accountability to the workers they claim to represent, and avoid restraints that are imposed on traditional labor organizations. Yet the laws that provide protections to workers, vis-a-vis labor organizations that represent them, were designed precisely to create that accountability.

Moreover, these laws were also intended to protect worker self-choice, to ensure a balance between labor and management, labor and management interests, and to ensure the free flow of commerce. The burden of compliance with those laws is not so severe, when considered within the context of the benefits afforded to workers and the economy in general. The mission of many worker centers is often seen as being an important means of advocating on behalf of underrepresented employees who do not have access to, or knowledge of, the legal mechanisms to protect their rights.

However, no organization, no matter how laudable its mission, is above reproach. And through its passage of laws that regulate labor organizations, Congress established safeguards to give workers a say in, and understanding of, the operations of the organizations that represent them. Compliance with the NLRA and LMRDA serves not only as a protection for workers, but perhaps as a validator of the worker centers that claim to represent them.

One goal of many worker centers is to ensure that employers of their members comply with the basic laws that offer protections to workers. Ultimately, the benefits of the laws that govern labor organizations flow to the workers they represent. And as such, there is simply no viable justification for worker centers not to comply with them.

Thank you for your time, and I look forward to answering any questions that you may have.

[The statement of Mr. Marculewicz follows:]

43

Testimony of Stefan Marculewicz Before

The United States House of Representatives

Health, Employment Labor and Pensions Subcommittee

September 19, 2013

Chairman Roe and Ranking Member Andrews, thank you for the opportunity to offer testimony to the members of this Committee. My name is Stefan Marculewicz and I am a Shareholder at the law firm of Littler Mendelson here in Washington, DC. I am speaking to you today on my own behalf and not on behalf of my firm or any firm client.

Labor unions, the primary advocates for workers' rights in the United States for more than a century, have experienced a significant decline in membership. As a result, labor unions have sought new and innovative means to effectuate change in the workplace.

One of the most significant examples of this effort is the development of organizations known as ''worker centers.'' In recent months, these groups have been involved in protests and other activities that have received substantial coverage in the media. Today there are hundreds of worker centers across the country. Their structure and composition vary. Typically, they are non-profit organizations that receive funding from foundations, grants-including from government, membership fees and other donations. Some are funded by other labor organizations. These groups offer a variety of services to their members, including education, training, employment services and legal advice. Increasingly, however, worker centers are directly engaging employers or groups of employers to effectuate change in the wages, hours and terms and conditions of workers they claim to represent. Indeed, when it comes to such direct engagement, these worker centers often act no differently than traditional labor organizations.

Yet, few of these groups comply with the laws that regulate labor organizations. Statutes like the National Labor Relations Act (NLRA) and the Labor Management Reporting and Disclosure Act (LMRDA) contain significant protections with respect to representational democracy, organizational democracy, access to basic information and promotion of a duty of fair representation. These basic rights are an important part of the process governing the representation of employees in the workplace by third-party organizations.

Even though compliance with these laws would confer benefits upon the very workers these groups claim to represent, many such groups are reluctant to define themselves as labor organizations because the NLRA and the LMRDA are perceived as creating an impediment to worker centers' activities. In addition, worker centers have not considered themselves to be limited by the NLRA restrictions on secondary picketing and protracted picketing for recognition, and such conduct is a common tool used by these groups to convey their message, although it would violate the NLRA.

Without coverage of the NLRA and LMRDA these organizations can avoid accountability to the workers they claim to represent and avoid restraints that are imposed on traditional labor organizations. Yet, the laws that provide protections to workers vis a vis labor organizations that represent them were designed precisely to create that accountability. Moreover, these laws were also intended to protect worker self-choice, to ensure a balance between labor and management interests, and to ensure the free flow of commerce. The burden of compliance with those laws is not so severe when considered within the context of the benefits afforded to workers and the economy in general.

The mission of many worker centers is often seen as being an important means of advocating on behalf of underrepresented employees who do not have access to or knowledge of the legal mechanisms to protect their rights. However, no organization, no matter how laudable its mission, is above reproach, and through its passage of the laws that regulate labor organizations, Congress established safeguards to give workers a say in and understanding of the operations of the organizations that represent them. Compliance with the NLRA and LMRDA serves not only as a protection for workers, but perhaps as a validator of the worker centers that claim to represent them.

A goal of many worker centers is to ensure that employers of their members comply with the basic laws that offer protections to workers. It therefore is not unreasonable to expect worker centers to do the same. Ultimately, the benefits of the laws that govern labor organizations flow to the workers they represent, and, as such, there simply is no viable justification for worker centers not to comply with them.

Thank you for your time, and I look forward to answering any questions you may have.

———

Chairman ROE. I thank the panel. And you all may be the best on the lights that I have seen since I have been here. Everybody was under the wire, so thank you all. You all did a great job.

I will now ask Mr. Salmon. Yield to him.

Mr. SALMON. Thank you. I appreciate the opportunity to listen to this panel's testimony. Thank you very much.

I have a little bit of a story, and I would like maybe some thoughts. Arizona had, really, only one family-owned grocery store left in Arizona, called Bashas'. The head of Bashas', who basically became the head of Bashas' after his father died, Eddie Basha, a very, very dear and close personal friend of mine. While I am a Republican, he was a prominent Democrat. In fact, about 15 years ago—might even be a little longer, maybe 18 years ago—he was the Democrat nominee for governor of the state of Arizona.

He didn't prevail. He ran against the incumbent. But Eddie has always been just a pillar in our community, always, you know, fighting for homeless people and against child abuse. Any good cause, Eddie was always there. And what is really tragic is that he was one of the top contributors, over the last, I would say, 30, 40 years to the Democrat Party and Democrat candidates. He was very prominent in the Democrat Party. And yet, time and time again the unions tried to organize at Bashas'.

And the employees themselves decided they didn't want to do it. So the last several years, they started resorting to some dirty tricks. In fact, they planted some overdue formula—some bad formula, baby formula—on the shelves, and they did all kinds of real nasty public relations tricks on him. In fact, they were caught red-handed on the planting of the tainted formula, or the overdue formula. And then they filed just multiple frivolous claims with the NLRB.

And they had an unlimited supply of money to file these lawsuits. And the upshot is that Eddie's company, Bashas', ended up going into bankruptcy because they had multimillion dollars of trying to defend against these stupid, frivolous lawsuits against the NLRB. And Eddie, much—sad to say, just in the last few months, passed away. But Arizona has sorely missed him.

My question is, what can be done to address some of these frivolous lawsuits and this aggressive tactic of just trying to wear somebody down through that kind of a process, to the point where they just either throw up their hands and give in or file bankruptcy like Bashas' had to? Any thoughts on that from anybody in the panel?

Mr. MEISBURG. I believe one thing that would help in these circumstances would be if the board would permit an employer to call for an election. In other words, make the fact that the employees don't want to join the union, make it a matter of record in a board election. And treat a corporate campaign of this sort like a demand for recognition. Now, the board has, in the past, had cases where they could do that. It has been bouncing around the board for a number of years.

I think that would let the employer say, "Listen, I am willing to let my employees decide whether they want to be a member—a union-represented shop or not. But I want to do it through a secret ballot election.'' Unless the union files for a petition or demands recognition, right now the employer can't make that happen. So what I think might help in those situations would be if the employer could say, ''Okay, I am willing to put this to a vote of my employees.''

And if there are a number of employees—the employees vote against it, then the union would be banned from—as they are trying to organize after a lost election for a year. And that would give, I think, some calming effect to these kinds of campaigns.

Mr. BURTON. I think the problem that you have identified is very real. Litigation costs can crush small businesses. Mr. Adams referred to how much money was being spent on lawyers. It is a problem throughout the entire legal system, not just NLRB. I think there is a need to streamline the procedures. Some of the things the NLRB has done along those lines makes sense, but a lot of them also do it in a way that don't really make sense.

But in the entire legal system, we have given some thought to the problem. And there is probably a need, at least with respect to smaller litigants that don't have unlimited resources. Fortune 500 companies and the federal government are fine, but small businesses and other smaller entities are not. To move more towards a small claims type arrangement or a continental European-type arrangement where the judge is more of a fact-finder rather than the two litigants being able to throw up walls and expend the other side's money on an almost unlimited basis in discovery or filing various motions.

These days, it can cost $60-to 100 grand to defend an utterly frivolous lawsuit. And that can be crushing to a small firm.

Chairman ROE. I thank the gentleman for yielding.

Mr. Andrews?

Mr. ANDREWS. Thank you, Mr. Chairman. I thank each of the witnesses for their testimony. Mr. Adams, thank you for serving our country and for being with us this morning. And thank all four of you.

It has now been, by my count, 601 days since Mr. Adams and his group won the organizing election he referred to. And, Mr. Adams, my understanding is there is still not a first contract. Is that right?

Mr. ADAMS. Yes, that is correct.

Mr. ANDREWS. Mr. Meisburg, on April 19 of 2006, in your role as general counsel, you wrote a memo. I want to read from it. You quote approvingly the federal mediation conciliation service, observing, ''Initial contract negotiations are often more difficult than established successor contract negotiations since they frequently follow contentious representation election campaigns.'' Then you go on to say, ''And when employees are bargaining for their first collective bargaining agreement, they are highly susceptible to unfair labor practices intended to undermine support for their bargaining representative.''

''Indeed, our records indicate that in the initial period after election and certification, charges alleging that employers that refuse to bargain are meritorious in more than a quarter of all newly-certified units, or 28 percent.'' That sounds like a sort of macro description of the case that Mr. Adams just talked about. What do you think we should do about these cases where there is a chronic failure to come to that first contract because of the kind of practices you discuss in 2006? What should we do to fix that problem?

Mr. MEISBURG. Well, what we did, at the time, was we followed up on that first contract bargaining initiative, which included a more aggressive use of 10–J, which is the injunction provisions of the act, which then can get into a situation where an employer can be in contempt. So that is a pretty powerful weapon. We also suggested other potential remedies that aren't typically used in board cases: bargaining on a specific schedule; reports by the employer directly to our regional directors about the status of the bargaining; and payment of the costs of the bargaining by the wrongful-acting party of the wronged party.

Mr. ANDREWS. Now, I know because of your recess status appointment situation, you weren't around for a whole long period of time to see this through. But did that tactic work?

Mr. MEISBURG. Well, that actually, I was there. I issued this memorandum before I was confirmed, and then I was confirmed.

Mr. ANDREWS. These days, that would be probably pretty smart—confirmation.

Mr. MEISBURG. And I followed up as a confirmed GC. What got me interested in it was, we noticed that——

Mr. ANDREWS. But did it work? Did the——

Mr. MEISBURG. Well, I think it did. And let me tell you statistics. When I first became GC, 50 percent of all the refusal to bargain, 85 bad faith bargaining charges were filed in first contract situations. When I left, that number had dropped to 25 percent. Now, I just felt like the arrows were pointing in the right direction when we left. Also, I think it is important to note—and this was in the last speech I gave as general counsel—80 percent of all first-contract bargaining succeeds without resort to the board.

Mr. ANDREWS. Yes——

Mr. MEISBURG. And that is a tribute to the——

Mr. ANDREWS. It is that 20 percent I am worried about.

Mr. Adams——

Mr. MEISBURG. I understand.

Mr. ANDREWS. Mr. Adams, what I want to ask Mr. Adams a question. There is a proposal that has been before the Congress that after a certain number of days if there wasn't a first contract there would be mediation, where your union and the company would have had to go to a mediator and talk about things. And after a certain number of days, if that didn't work the first contracts could be subject to what is called ''binding arbitration,'' where you guys would make your offer, the company would make its offer, and the arbitrator would choose the outcome that he or she thought was best.

Would that have helped you in this situation?

Mr. ADAMS. Tremendously, it would have helped a lot. In fact, I would already be within the first year of an actual contract had that been in place.

Mr. ANDREWS. It is interesting that if you played for the Yankees, which you probably could—if you played for the Yankees and you had that situation, you would get that kind of arbitrator. Because, in other words, you would have the bargaining leverage to have somebody figure out what you were worth. So you would support a proposal in the law that would, after a certain period of time, provide for that binding arbitration.

Mr. ADAMS. Absolutely, yes.

Mr. ANDREWS. Thank you very much.

Chairman ROE. I thank the gentleman for yielding.

Mr. Guthrie?

Mr. GUTHRIE. Thank you. Thanks for all the panelists for being here. And, Mr. Adams, I thank you for your service and willing to put on the uniform and serve overseas. I was actually in Brooklyn Monday. I went to college in metro New York, at West Point. And so Brooklyn has changed a lot. It is great, it is a wonderful place. I enjoyed being there. So it was wonderful to be there. It has changed a lot since the 1980s, so it was great to be there.

But I have a question for Mr. Burton. You mentioned in your testimony, and I have heard from small businesses, about the persuader activity. And from my own experience, I know the importance of being able to seek outside counsel. So I would like you to—give you a chance to expand on the persuader rule a little bit. And you mentioned specifically in testimony that imposing additional burdens on employers seeking advice would be a deterrent to seeking advice.

And could you expand on that for just a couple of minutes. I have another question of another panelist, but—about the persuader activity and how it will discourage people from seeking advice.

Mr. BURTON. Okay. Well, if you end up having to buy into a bureaucratic morass, filing reports, and then potentially having to spend a great deal of money to hire people to advise you how to fill out the reports, then you will tend not to want to hire consultants. Because they don't cost just what you have to pay them, but——

Mr. GUTHRIE. You know what the——

Mr. BURTON.—the entire compliance cost associated with it.

Mr. GUTHRIE. You know what the Department of Labor is trying to get to in that rule, and why you think they are wrong in that?

Mr. BURTON. I am not entirely sure what their true rationale is. I think part of it is so that they can obtain information that they would find useful in terms of understanding better the employer strategy in unionization campaigns. And also would—this, of course, would not be lawful, but some might want to use it for purposes of intimidating people.

Mr. GUTHRIE. Well, thank you for that. And I have a question for Mr. Marculewicz? Is that correct? Under both the NLRA and LMRDA, one of the primary elements in determining whether an entity is a labor organization is whether it exists for the purpose, in whole or part, of dealing with employers concerning terms and conditions of employment. Last month, in response to an oversight letter sent by this committee, the Department of Labor stated it concluded, in 2004 and 2008, that the restaurant opportunity center was not a labor organization primarily because it did not deal, or intend to deal, with employers.

How have the courts defined "dealing with?" Is the department's conclusion consistent with your findings related to RLC?

48

Mr. MARCULEWICZ. Thank you. The concept of—well, first and foremost, the concept of worker centers has evolved dramatically in the last 5 years. We have seen a tremendous amount of activity by these groups, and they have engaged in a wide variety of different things. The situation that occurred in 2004 and 2008 with respect to those letters, the analysis under the Labor-Management Reporting and Disclosure Act provides that it has to be an organization in which employees participate, that it have a purpose, in whole or in part, of dealing with an employer over issues related to wages, hours, and terms and conditions of employment.

The definition of that "dealing with" is pretty—the bar is set very, very low. And, in fact, the National Labor Relations Board has the same test for employer-created committees, and has found many of those committees to be violative of section 882 of the National Labor Relations Act when an employer creates an organization that engages in a dialogue and engages in, you know, so dealing with their workforce. And as a result of that, it is a fairly low bar.

And, in fact, the NLRB has reached—has considered a number of cases where the name of the case is actually Group of Concerned Workers and Their Leader. Because they have grouped together, engaged in picketing or other activity, and the NLRB has looked at that and said, you know, they have a goal of dealing with, their purpose is dealing with, it is focused on the intent. And if you look at some of the activities of these worker centers subsequent to that, you will see that—you know, I think there is a wide variety of attempts to effectuate change in the workplace.

Mr. GUTHRIE. I am about to run out of time. So also on that, you mentioned that because they are not limited that they do secondary picketing. And what is secondary picketing, and why does the NRLA respect secondary picketing and protracted picketing for recognition?

Mr. MARCULEWICZ. Secondary picketing is where, if you and I have a labor dispute and one of my major customers—you go and picket that major customer—that customer has nothing to do with our labor dispute, the NLRB prohibits that, or the National Labor Relations Act prohibits, that secondary—they are trying to protect the true neutrals; those who are not interested to—and it was Congress' balance of the balance of the interests of labor and management and the pursuit of the free flow of commerce.

Mr. GUTHRIE. So the work centers are doing the secondary picketing.

Mr. MARCULEWICZ. In many situations. Not all, but in many situations, yes.

Mr. GUTHRIE. I believe I am out of time.

I yield back.

Chairman ROE. Mr. Grijalva?

Mr. GRIJALVA. Thank you, Mr. Chairman. Let me ask Mr. Adams a couple of questions, if I may. And as a point of reference to my friend and colleague from Arizona, and the comments regarding Bashas', the grocery chain, a very large grocery chain in Arizona. Mr. Basha, who passed is a good philanthropist, great immigrant story. And considered him a friend.

But at the same time, the lawsuits that were referenced and some of the other issues dealt with some very specific things: OSHA violations worker safety. It also dealt with violations of overtime. It also dealt with other kinds of issues that any individual employee has the right to, and should, exercise that right. And exercising the right does not make the people doing that, or the organization helping with that, necessarily evil. And I would subject— I would ask people that there is, in any question of that magnitude, there is always another side.

Let me ask Mr. Adams, in your testimony you—well, let me go— in your testimony, you said that the management at Cablevision had no intention of bargaining. Can you share some of the tactics they used to pressure, intimidate workers, and really keep from formalizing what, through election, the workers wanted to sit down and collectively bargain?

Mr. ADAMS. Thank you. One of the things that my coworkers and I definitely noticed is, they were obviously objectionable to the whole of us unionizing in the first place. They didn't think it was necessary. One of the things we tried to point out to management is that there was a serious need for structure. A lot of the times there was a lot of, you know, favoritism, things like that, that go on. And it is unfair to a number of employees who are doing the right thing and, you know, following some of the expectations that the company has for, you know, the employees.

One of the things that I have noticed—especially last year, the number of meetings we had, their way of trying to inform us what was best for us was to tell us that we didn't need to form a union. Are we—you know, are we sure that we know what we are getting into. And no matter how often we made them aware of the fact that we were very sure and this was what we wanted to do, they always seemed to come up with a new way of trying to derail it.

I have to say, this is, without question, one of the hardest things that I have ever been through. As you know already, I have been fired already. Myself and 21 other employees were fired because we basically took advantage of an open door policy to speak with management on the morning of January 30. It would have only literally taken about 5 minutes. They were very dismissive. They seemed to have other things to do.

And like I said, they—you know, Mr. Levesque invited us, the vice president of our shop invited us into the room. And he basically told us we were all being permanently replaced. That was just one of the things that took place to try to intimidate the workers. As soon as we were led out by police escort and we were removed from the building, a memo went out to the employees about decertification.

A lot of the employees, already intimidated by the fact that a number of the stronger members were already led out the door, got them to feel like they didn't have a chance against Cablevision. And so a lot of them felt like they had to put their names on the paper to decertify.

Mr. GRIJALVA. Open door policies that the company has. What else is covered other than coming in and stating your opinion to management? What else is covered in that policy?

Mr. ADAMS. If there is any general concerns that we have, one of the things that is covered in there, especially when it comes to employee safety—you know, there are a lot of times that we have to do things that are otherwise unsafe. You know, it is not really safe for the employee to do. We are climbing rooftops, fire escapes, you know, we are in backyards where most people, you know, traditionally don't have much traffic.

A lot of the time people do get hurt, and they end up, you know, being off the job for some time, sometimes over 4 or 5, 6 months. You know, Cablevision has already, this past year, two employees were let go because they weren't able to recover in time from their injuries. A lot of the times employees feel the need to come in and work, you know, sometimes with injuries, you know, that are work-related. And they refuse to let management know about it because they understand that they will not be able to relate to what is going on with them, or at least do the right thing in making sure they take care of those employees.

Mr. GRIJALVA. Thank you. And, Mr. Chairman, with regard to the comments on the worker centers, it should be noted that much of the activity and support these centers are providing is to immigrant workers all across this country, including the push for an increased minimum wage. And, in doing so, are providing a service, providing English lessons, providing social services, and providing a voice to a group of workers in this country that have historically been exploited.

And I would consider that a good thing for the overall economy of this country and, certainly, for those immigrant workers' rights.

With that, I yield back.

Chairman ROE. I thank the gentleman for yielding.

Mr. Miller?

Mr. MILLER. Thank you. And I want to thank Mr. Adams for coming and testifying today. I also want to recognize Lana Stuart and Tanya Cauley, who are in our audience today. I have had many of my constituents participate in our Wal-Mart—and my conversations with them in my office and on the street, a lot of it about just they are trying to figure out—you know, they know that with Wal-Mart discussion of a union is toxic.

They are trying to figure out how to keep their job, and how they get some respect and how they get a decent wage and how they get decent conditions in working, and don't live in a place of intimidation. I mean, Wal-Mart has figured it out pretty clearly. They have the highest paid truck drivers in the country. Because they know if they don't the Teamsters can organize them. But people on the floor, they are interchangeable.

Just fire them and find somebody else to do that job, as hard as it is and as difficult as it is. And that is, you know—and so if you try to figure it out yourself among your peers, you can get fired. If you talk to somebody from OUR[MG3] Wal-Mart, you can get fired. So you can be arbitrary as hell in that fashion. But if you then go the other route, as Mr. Adams went, you spend a year trying to talk to your coworkers and get a union and you win an election. What did you win by, Mr. Adams, 180 to 86?

Mr. ADAMS. Yes, that is correct.

Mr. MILLER. Yes. Everybody that gets elected, close the deal. Except your deal never got closed.

Mr. ADAMS. That is correct, yes.

Mr. MILLER. So now you have spent how long? What is it—Mr. Andrews says 600 days?

Mr. ADAMS. Six-hundred-one.

Mr. MILLER. Six-hundred-one days trying to get the results of your election.

Mr. ADAMS. Yes.

Mr. MILLER. And get the benefits of the bargaining. Which I understand started out with you are asking for parity.

Mr. ADAMS. Yes.

Mr. MILLER. And I assume if you find out that this unit can crawl and walk and run, you might ask for something else some day.

Mr. ADAMS. Hopefully, we will be able to get a contract.

Mr. MILLER. Yes.

[Laughter.]

Mr. ADAMS. Hopefully.

Mr. MILLER. So they don't give you the contract, and Mr. Andrews went through that part of it. And they gave everybody around you a raise, but not for the people in your unit that signed up for the union.

Mr. ADAMS. That is correct.

Mr. MILLER. So Mr. Dolan can be as arbitrary and as capricious as he wants to be, as long as you don't get a contract.

Mr. ADAMS. That is correct.

Mr. MILLER. So he can reward people, trying to send a signal to the 186 that joined you that they just missed out on this benefit of—what was it you said, $5,000 to 25,000, something like that. I didn't get the benefit of your previous testimony, but.

Mr. ADAMS. Upwards of $27,000, yes, $18,000.

Mr. MILLER. So just a cash benefit.

Mr. ADAMS. Yep.

Mr. MILLER. Telling people to stay away from this unit. And then I guess this progressive company, Cablevision, they have an open door policy.

Mr. ADAMS. Yes. Yes, they do. They have an open door policy.

Mr. MILLER. Unless you are in the union, it turns out to be a trapdoor.

Mr. ADAMS. Pretty much.

Mr. MILLER. Yes. So you must be wondering where you go to get justice.

Mr. ADAMS. I am, actually. My and——

Mr. MILLER. Where do you go to get your union. And these people can drag you out for 600 days. They can fire you because you asked for a 5-minute meeting. Apparently, you didn't even ask for a meeting in front of other workers. You asked for a meeting with your group, with him, with Mr. Levesque is it?

Mr. ADAMS. Rick Levesque, yes.

Mr. MILLER. And that meeting, that meeting got you permanently displaced, or immediately replaced.

Mr. ADAMS. That is correct. Permanently replaced, yes.

Mr. MILLER. You need a union.

52

Mr. MILLER. That is what—because these people are about as arbitrary and capricious as an employer could be. And this is just, you know, a company that is a rogue with respect to its employees. They have decided also that you are replaceable. And anybody else that, apparently, speaks up, uses their policies, uses the law, can be punished and lose their job and lose the benefits of an increase in pay. And they are daring you to do something about it.

Mr. ADAMS. That is correct.

Mr. MILLER. It is really unfortunate for you. You know, and I noticed several members here thank you for your service to the country. Don't make a damn bit of difference when you are in that workplace at Cablevision. Doesn't make a damn bit of difference. Made a big difference to us as a country and to your fellow servicepeople.

Thank you very much for your testimony.

Mr. ADAMS. Thank you.

Chairman ROE. Mr. Courtney?

Mr. COURTNEY. Thank you, Mr. Chairman. I actually just wanted to pick up where Mr. Miller left off. You testified, Mr. Adams, that what you have been going through is the toughest thing you have ever experienced?

Mr. ADAMS. Yes, that is correct.

Mr. COURTNEY. Okay. And you are a U.S. Marine combat veteran of Iraq. Is that correct?

Mr. ADAMS. Yes. Support, yes.

Mr. COURTNEY. Yes. And when you entered the Marines you entered as a volunteer. Isn't that correct?

Mr. ADAMS. Yes.

Mr. COURTNEY. And you took an oath. And in that oath, you swore to uphold the Constitution and the laws of this country, is that correct?

Mr. ADAMS. Yes, that is correct.

Mr. COURTNEY. And when we go into military service, again, you are not taking an oath to an individual or to the homeland or to the motherland. You are really taking an oath to a system that is about protecting people's dignity and rights as American citizens. Isn't that correct?

Mr. ADAMS. Yes, that is correct.

Mr. COURTNEY. And it—again, I just—you know, listening to this—your story, it just is stunning to see that, you know, where you were prepared to put your life on the line as a Marine, and to come and have the system, again, really just trample on your rights. Which, again, are not sort of just statutory rights. The rights to collectively bargain are recognized by the United Nations human rights charter. It was recognized by Pope Leo in the Vatican in the late 1880s in terms of—1880s, in terms of recognizing that human dignity is tied to the fact that people have the right to withhold their work as a way of bargaining for appropriate working conditions.

And yet you are in a situation now where 600 days after going through the process, following the rules, obeying the law, that, again, you still do not have an outcome that the law claims to offer. Isn't that correct?

Mr. ADAMS. Yes, that is correct.

53

Mr. COURTNEY. The Marines actually have a motto. Isn't that correct?

Mr. ADAMS. Yes, they do.

Mr. COURTNEY. And what is it?

Mr. ADAMS. "Always Faithful—Semper Fi."

Mr. COURTNEY. Semper Fi. Well, there is also another Latin term called ubi jus ibi remedium, which says that "without a remedy, there is no right." And, again, that is first-year law class, you know, taught to individuals. Marshall v. Marbury, that was the principle that the U.S. Supreme Court, establishing its authority, enunciated. And it is a very simple concept. Which is that, you know, you can have all the platitudes in the world about people's right to equality and votes and collective bargaining. But if you don't have a remedy, it really doesn't exist.

And what your story proves is that the decline in union membership, which we have heard from witnesses and which we have heard from the chairman, is frankly because we have a broken system. And sadly, in this committee room, you know, we have seen measures brought forth trying to exploit the fact that the filibuster rule was used in the Senate to basically neuter the National Labor Relations Board and use that. Not the merits of cases, but use that procedure as a device to, again, basically strip people of their rights.

Thank goodness, they are—you know, the majority leader exercised a procedural measure to make sure that we now have a fully-staffed National Labor Relations Board. But the fact of the matter is, you know, that just sort of gets us to the point where we can begin the process of making sure that situations like yours are addressed. So thank you for your amazing service, for you belief in our system. Not just as a soldier, but also a citizen and as a worker.

And, again, we—and some of us here want to make sure that we create a system that really balances rights and remedies so that people can actually have available to them—which is, again, bedrock human rights principles that has been recognized by international organizations and, in fact, the Vatican.

I yield back.

Chairman ROE. I thank the gentleman for yielding.

Ms. Wilson?

Ms. WILSON. Thank you, Mr. Chair. Strengthening labor means strengthening our economy. And according to the Bureau of Labor Statistics, the median weekly earnings of full-time union workers in 2012 were $943 compared with $742 for non-union workers, or $10,400 per year per worker. So people who are in unions earn less than people who are not. By getting more income into the hands of hardworking people who will spend it, we ensure more customers for American businesses and eliminate much of the need for government assistance.

This is the case now more than ever. At a time of high unemployment and falling living standards for workers, today a parent working full-time at minimum wage will simply not earn enough income to cover basic needs like food, clothing and shelter. Even working a second job and well over 40 years a week, it is mathematically impossible for many minimum wage workers to pay for child care,

54

clothing and gas. If you doubt these claims, take a look at the draft budget that a major employer distributed to its employees.

According to a new study from the Economic Policy Institute, the bottom 60 percent of workers are earning less than they did 13 years ago. According to a recent report by the Center for Economic & Policy Research, black Americans who have earned much higher average levels of education over recent decades have a lower chance of earning a living wage today than they had 30 years ago. And so economic growth remains slow, unemployment stays high, government debt continues to grow.

My question to Mr. Adams—and I have read your story, and I commend you for your bravery and for standing tall for working men and women—and I would like for you to—I would like to find out your view. How does collective bargaining affect low-and middle class Americans' purchasing power?

Mr. ADAMS. Well, what it does is, it definitely helps, at least for the people who have already gone through the experience of earning low incomes, it really helps a lot when it comes to being able to pay rent, being able to provide, you know, medical, being able to just get some of the common items that every American deserves and as to be as comfortable as possible, to work hard as possible, and to earn a reasonable salary.

With collective bargaining, what it does is, it just points out that the workers, if they have a good structure, are able to, you know, help the company, you know, strive where it needs to go. And then at the same time, without—I could—I don't—I hate to use the term, without "greed" being part of the equation. Where everybody is doing well, normally you would get, obviously, better results. Better workers, people are willing to go the extra mile. And with collective bargaining, it allows both sides to at least be able to, you know, review that. And like I said—and it helps families tremendously.

Ms. WILSON. Yes. Well, you keep up the good fight. I have always been a strong supporter of unions. I come from the public school sector, where unions play a major role in making sure that there is equal pay for everyone working for the school system. So it is a bargaining procedure to make sure that people receive health care, the benefits that they need to keep people at least surviving and not falling below the poverty level.

And I just can't even imagine what we would actually do in our school district in Miami-Dade County if we did not have the support of the unions making sure that people received a wage commensurate with what their living demanded. So thank you for keeping on the—stay on the path.

Mr. ADAMS. Thank you.

Chairman ROE. I thank the gentlelady for yielding.

Dr. DesJarlais?

Mr. DESJARLAIS. Thank you, Mr. Chairman. And thank you all for being here today. I would like to start with Mr. Marculewicz. If a worker center is a labor organization under federal law, what are the filing requirements and restrictions on activity?

Mr. MARCULEWICZ. Well, as in any labor organization they must file an LM–1, which is a form with the Department of Labor that incorporates and includes the constitution and bylaws. And this is designed to provide disclosure, public information to those who have an interest in that. Specifically those who are seeking to be— you know, or that group is seeking to represent as to how officers are elected, what the process is, and the like.

There are also financial disclosures, in an LM–2—or if you are a smaller labor organization, an LM–4—which are forms that are filed with the Department of Labor that incorporate references and describe and disclose the information, financial information, for the labor organization. So workers, members can understand where the money is coming from and where the money is going.

Mr. DESJARLAIS. Okay. I think you have partially answered this, but why are the filing requirements and restrictions so important?

Mr. MARCULEWICZ. Well, they are important because back when the Labor-Management Reporting and Disclosure Act was enacted by Congress there were really fundamental problems of corruption within labor unions. The McClellan hearings, which took place—actually were the first televised, to my understanding the first televised hearings in congressional history. And there was a fair amount of interest in the issue. And it exposed union corruption, exposed a wide variety of issues related to that.

And the law was passed to ensure that workers who were members and represented by these groups had a democratic right of participation, a right to expression of opinion, a right to vote. I mean, they have to elect their leadership, in a local, every 3 years and in an international every 5 years. And those democratic principles are sort of at the foundation of organizational representation.

Mr. DESJARLAIS. Okay, thank you. Where do worker centers get their funding?

Mr. MARCULEWICZ. Typically, worker centers—they get them, as I indicated in my initial remarks, they receive funding from a wide variety of sources. There are grants. Foundations will make contributions to them. There are also government grants that can be— that they can apply for and they can obtain. They also—some of them also receive direct funding from labor organizations. So the money comes from a variety of different sources.

Now, the reality is, is that there is no disclosure related to where that money comes from if that worker center doesn't consider itself a labor organization. Now, recognize this. That workers—not all worker centers act like labor organizations, but many of them are starting to do so. And that is—once you become a labor organization and start engaging in dealing with an employer, there is a responsibility to file that and to disclose that information.

Mr. DESJARLAIS. Okay. Does this affect their tax status?

Mr. MARCULEWICZ. Well, typically—there is actually a very good piece written by Diana Furchtgott Roth on the worker center tax treatment. And typically, a labor organization is a 501(c)(5) organization, which has different type—it is a different type of tax treatment. But many worker centers file, or designate themselves, as 501(c)(3)s. And the manner in which you can contribute is different. There are also contribution limitations by employers under the Labor-Management Relations Act. Section 302 also limits how money can be given to these worker centers.

Mr. DESJARLAIS. Thank you, sir.

The next question will be for Mr. Meisburg. In fiscal year 2011, labor unions won more than 71 percent of representation elections; 89 percent of those elections were held pursuant to agreements of the union and employer, commonly referred to as voluntary consent agreements. The median time to proceed to an election from the filing of a petition was 38 days. It appears the NLRB elections are timely, and unions fare pretty well. In rare cases, the time between a petition election can be significantly longer. What is the source of these elections' delay?

Mr. MEISBURG. Well, I haven't done a study of that personally. But my experience suggests that a lot of the delay is caused in blocking charge cases. I know I had one case where we—it was between the SCIU and the NUHW in California. And there was a petition for an election by the NUHW which was blocked for over a year by a charge filed by the SEIU. Eventually, we refused to issue a complaint. The block was withdrawn.

Now, the block can be withdrawn by a regional director if the permission of the board at other times. But my sense is, and without having made a study, a thorough study of is, that is the source of a lot of delay in, and it skews the statistics higher in those cases.

Mr. DESJARLAIS. Is this the exception to the rule?

Mr. MEISBURG. It is. I mean, you know——

Chairman ROE. The gentleman is time has expired.

Mr. DESJARLAIS. Oh, sorry, Mr. Chairman.

Chairman ROE. Dr. Holt?

Mr. HOLT. I thank the chair. I would like to address Mr. Adams. I was pleased to meet you in Brooklyn. I am impressed by your service. I would think that the customers of the company must be very pleased to know that someone such as you, so thoughtful and diligent, is on the job. And as a policymaker, I must say I am very pleased to find someone who so articulately expresses the worker's point of view.

You know, for well over half a century now labor laws in this country have protected workers who believe that a union, through collective bargaining, can improve their working conditions and safety and pay and benefits. And those protections, I think, have been well-justified because, over the intervening decades, unions have, and to this day continue to be, I think, continue to have a very beneficial effect on working conditions and safety and pay and benefits.

What we see, and I have looked at this pretty closely, what we see there with the Cablevision instance is a textbook example of what has come to be known as union busting. In punishment, in your case firing, for those who want to organize; inducements to try to entice others not to organize; all sorts of statements, and then retractions of those statements, and delays right up to the deadlines. It is a textbook example of how you use or misuse the laws to prevent unionization. And even to this very day, the corporation is spending millions of dollars to continue to fight this. Far more than was at stake in the salaries and in the pay under dispute.

You have spoken about, we have heard about, Cablevision CEO, Jim Dolan's visit to the Bronx field technicians who were getting ready to vote on affiliating and organizing. And he said they would be left behind in training and investment and promotion and job

57

advancement. And that group did not vote to affiliate. How do you distinguish that from what happened with your group of field technicians? And from what you know about the Employee Free Choice Act, how would that have made a difference in the Bronx? How would it have made it a difference for your group?

Mr. ADAMS. Well, one of the things that would have been extremely beneficial, at least, you know, for the technicians in the Bronx, when Mr. Dolan went to go visit them he did so simply because he realized that by underestimating the technicians in Brooklyn he decided to, obviously, do something that would otherwise, like I say, point to our being irresponsible, so to speak, by being a bit manipulative with his message. It was very difficult to get the truth out to the Bronx.

Like I said, Cablevision has an unlimited amount of resources. Like I said before, they have over 60 lawyers already working on this case. They are spending countless amount of money just trying to stop something that—I can't understand why—but to stop something that we have already, like I said, strongly made a decision on. I just think that if, had we had the Free Choice Act, like I said, I would already be one year into our first contract. And then possibly at least coming together to make an even better second one.

Because that is what I honestly thought this was all gonna be about. Just being able to create better structure, to basically let them know that obviously he proved us correct by paying the other workers more money to help better their situations. When those things are being brought up, that is really what we were hoping that Mr. Dolan and his management team would see. That obviously we were behind. So had that been in place, this would all be behind us and, like I said, we would be already one year into our first contract.

Mr. HOLT. Thank you. And Mr. Chairman, I understand 55 percent of the workers still support the union, which is about equal to the original..

[Off mike.]

Mr. ADAMS. That is correct.

Mr. HOLT. [Off mike.]

Chairman ROE. The gentleman's time has expired and I appreciate the gentleman yielding.

I will now yield myself 5 minutes. And Mr. Meisburg, if you would like to continue your thoughts.

Mr. MEISBURG. Well, just at the end of that last question I had about whether it was typical for blocking charges to be filed, they are—it is not typical. It happens, but it is not the rule, I don't believe.

Chairman ROE. Yes, I thank you.

And now, Mr. Burton, and I agree with Dr. Holt that basically, as I understand, the NLRA was passed, I think, in 1935. And then the NLRB was established to be a fair arbiter between the employees and employers. So that you didn't favor either side. It is like being in a ball game, where you go and you hope the refs are fair. And you want a—you just want a fair hearing. When some people run the string out or whatever, they are at the tail—most of time, as I understand these, the unions win most elections, 71 percent.

The elections are—and this happens in a fairly timely fashion. I think within less than a month and a week, 35 days, I believe is the median. So it seems like that it allows both sides to get—a small business especially—to get the expertise in. I was thinking about my own business. I wouldn't have any idea how to go out and find a labor lawyer. I would have to go find somebody if I—and I couldn't do it in 10 days or 15 days. It is impossible.

So both sides need to be fair. And this case that Mr. Adams points out probably is at the other end of the scale. So I want to ask a couple of questions about—for you, Mr. Burton. And the statistics to the size of our units, they fluctuate year-to-year. And there is a graph over here that is up. And the Democrats are correct that the median size of units has increased from 2011 to 2012. However, the average size—there is a difference between median and average—has decreased from 71 to 65 in 2012.

And these are interesting numbers, but they really don't address the issue of Specialty Health Care where this is the fragmentation of the workforce. That is what I want to ask the question. And also Bergdorf Goodman you mentioned. How does fragmentation of the workforce affect the employers and employees? And number two, can you give me an example of workplace fragmentation by recent NLRB unit certification?

Mr. BURTON. Well, fragmentation is a problem in the sense that you could end up having to deal with many unions. You can have some aspects of your company governed by one collective bargaining agreement, and another. And there is a multiplicity of agreements, a multiplicity of unions, complexity, inability to move back and forth and so on down the line. The case that I mentioned briefly in my oral remarks is, to me, the most dramatic—the Bergdorf case, where you are organizing by shoe department, a department store.

There is another case that, out of the Northrop Grumman cited in my written statement, where I believe they organized 180 out of 2,400 technicians in the shipyard. So you end up having a lot of division. I think that the—and it was all launched by specialty health care which, of course, is a specific job description type unit. This is of concern to small employers, but not really small employers. Mid-size, 100, 200 type employers, which is part of our membership base.

Chairman ROE. Next question would be, in your experience, and anybody can answer this, when do employers become aware that—of a union organizing drive? And anyone can—how do you know when you are being organized?

Mr. BURTON. Well, that can vary dramatically. Sometimes it can be reported to you by employees. But obviously, sometimes people find out about it when the petition is filed by the labor union. So it just varies dramatically. The one thing I think that is most important to understand is, most small employers don't know anything about labor law until they have to. They know about employment law, or maybe NRLA section 7 rights of like social media or what have you.

But they don't know about unions or union organizing. The unions generally do. That is what they do for a living. Six-hundred days is ridiculous. Ten days is also ridiculous. I mean, there needs to be a reasonable middle ground found. But there is no way on God's green earth that a typical small business owner is going to be able to find representation, understand the law, understand the implications for his business, explain it to his employees, and adequately present the facts to his employees in 10 days.

Chairman ROE. Yes. I will now cut myself off. I would like to again thank the witnesses for taking time to testify before the committee. Y'all have been a terrific group.

I will now recognize the ranking member for closing statements.

Mr. ANDREWS. Well, I, too, want to thank the witnesses and our fellow members for their participation this morning. I think we heard a lot of good information. I wanted to come back to one thing Mr. Meisburg said which struck a chord with me. Which is that whatever ideological or political disputes may happen, it is very important that the dedicated career employees of the National Labor Relations Board be respected in the integrity of their work. And I appreciate that.

And again, I—this is just my own observation. I am not putting words in anyone's mouth. But one of the things that we were disturbed about previously—and Mr. Miller, Mr. Cummings and Mr. Conyers wrote a letter on August 12 of 2011—when the dispute over the Boeing case was going on and the board had filed a complaint against Boeing, there was a subpoena served on the board by the—not by this committee, by the Government Reform Committee, that called for all communications that took place between the regional office and the board pertaining to the filing of the Boeing complaint.

Now, obviously, that was a rather hotly-contested item. But one of the things we were worried about then was that the trial strategy, the negotiated settlement strategy, the work that the regional office was doing was gonna be subject to invasion in a public forum. And I think that was a grave concern. So I thought about that, Mr. Meisburg, when you made that remark. I know that was not your intention, but it triggered that response with me.

And I take it as a worthy admonition. The NLRB is a place where there are fierce ideological battles. It has been this way for a very long time. I hoped that we could bridge some of them. But certainly, the work of the men and women in the regional offices and in the main office, the career people, should not be abridged in any way. And I think that was a very important point that you made.

Mr. Chairman, I think this panel has served us well. I appreciate their time and effort. Mr. Adams, we especially appreciate your efforts, as well. And we thank you for your time.

Chairman ROE. I thank the gentleman for yielding. And I thank the panel. And in closing, you know, we have, in this country right now, a real problem with jobs. And we have had a huge problem. And you have noticed that the jobs in unions have dropped from 20 percent of the population down to around 7 in the private sector. I grew up in a union household. My dad worked in a factory, made shoe heels. He belonged to the union as—after World War II until he died. And died before he was able to retire.

So we have some issues. The ranking member and myself are gonna work on union issues with pensions. It is a huge issue. We plan to work diligently on that to help save those. I believe, quite frankly, that we will not recreate the middle class in America until we recreate—bring manufacturing back to this country. There are estimates out there, with a coherent energy policy in this country— if we had just exactly like President Kennedy did when I was a high school student, he said we are going to go to the moon in this decade. And we beat that.

Americans are that good. We beat that deadline. We put somebody on the moon in less than 10 years. We can become energy independent in America, if we use all the resources we have, within 10 years. And Mr. Adams, one of the reasons that I have to look at energy independence, it was 40 years ago this year I was stationed just south of the DMZ in Korea. And I almost froze to death because we only got heat 3 hours a day.

And the reason was because the Middle East embargoed our oil and we had to keep the oil for our Huey—fuel for our Huey helicopters, our Cobra gunships, our tanks and so forth. And you understand that very well. We were a hostage of what somebody else halfway around the world did. If I could be the President of the United States for 1 month—and I don't want to be, but if I were— in 1 month——

Mr. ANDREWS. You are announcing your candidacy?

Chairman ROE. No.

[Laughter.]

Mr. ANDREWS. Okay, all right.

Chairman ROE. Trust me, I already said I don't want to be. But I would have a coherent energy policy so that I think—for middle America, where I grew up, the price of energy affects us more than anything. You see a gallon of gas go up a dollar. That affects everybody. When they have got to fill their tank up where we live and drive miles to their job, if they are making $10 or $11 or $12 an hour it may take an entire day's work just to get to and from work.

And that is why we have to do that. And there are estimates out there, with people a lot smarter than I am, that say in the next 8 to 10 years we can create 2–1/2 to 5 million manufacturing jobs if we become energy independent. And let me tell you, the American worker is the best worker in the world. And I was in China a year—a little over a year ago. And it struck me when I was in Beijing, you know they have done a lot of building. You hear all about China.

That country has 1.4 billion, with a "B," people. The United States of America has 300 million people, and we produce more goods and services than they do. The best worker in the world in the American, and the most productive. We have got to give them the tools in which to do that. And I really think recreation of the middle class will solve a lot of these problems for us going forward. I am concerned. Right now, I have got to share some real frustration with me in my job right now.

I spent 30 years, over 30 years practicing medicine. There is one hospital system in my state that because of what is going on in health care right now is going to have to make a $250 million cut. We have just lost 50 residency slots, how we train young doctors in the community I live in Johnson City, Tennessee. This is going on all over the country, the effects of the Affordable Care Act. We need to step back and re-look at that.

It is affecting the economy. We have had a hospital close in southwest Virginia, very close. It will close the 1st of October, this year. I look forward to working with you all. I appreciate very much all of the input from the members. And you all did a great job. I appreciate you being here.

With no further business, this hearing is adjourned.

[Whereupon, at 11:37 a.m., the subcommittee was adjourned.]

APPENDIX

———

MATERIAL SUBMITTED FOR THE HEARING RECORD

NATIONAL
RESTAURANT
ASSOCIATION

September 18, 2013

The Honorable John Kline
Chairman
Committee on Education and the
Workforce
U.S. House of Representatives
Washington, D.C. 20515

The Honorable Phil Roe
Chairman
Subcommittee on Health, Employment,
Labor, and Pensions
U.S. House of Representatives
Washington, D.C. 20515

Re: Support for Efforts to Examine the Future of Labor Organizing

Dear Chairman Kline and Chairman Roe:

On behalf of the National Restaurant Association, we thank you for calling attention to the increasingly blurred line between "so-called 'worker centers' and labor organizations." We are encouraged by the hearing scheduled for tomorrow, September 19, 2013, on "The Future of Labor Organizing."

The National Restaurant Association is the leading business association for the restaurant and food service industry. The industry is comprised of 980,000 restaurant and foodservice outlets employing 13.1 million people who serve 130 million guests daily. Despite being an industry of predominately small businesses, the restaurant industry is the nation's second-largest private-sector employer, employing about 10 percent of the U.S. workforce.

The Labor-Management Reporting and Disclosure Act (LMRDA) contains a number of annual filing requirements meant to bring transparency and clarity with regard to organizations "in which employees participate and which exists for the purpose, in whole or in part, of dealing with employers concerning grievances, labor disputes, wages, rates of pay, hours, or other terms or condition of employment." Some of these groups even admit to "using tactics that include organizing workers," but somehow fail to abide by the requirements of the LMRDA.

We appreciate the Committee's efforts and thank you for examining this critical issue.

Sincerely,

Angelo I. Amador, Esq.
Vice President
Labor & Workforce Policy

Ryan P. Kearney
Manager
Labor & Workforce Policy

Cc: Members of the House Subcommittee on Health, Employment, Labor, and Pensions

**Associated Builders
and Contractors, Inc.**

September 19, 2013

The Honorable Phil Roe   The Honorable Rob Andrews
Chairman   Ranking Member
Subcommittee on Health, Employment,   Subcommittee on Health, Employment,
Labor and Pensions   Labor and Pensions
Committee on Education and the Workforce   Committee on Education and the Workforce
U.S. House of Representatives   U.S. House of Representatives
Washington, DC 20515   Washington, DC 20515

Dear Chairman Roe and Ranking Member Andrews:

On behalf of Associated Builders and Contractors (ABC), a national trade association with 72 chapters representing nearly 22,000 members from more than 19,000 construction and industry-related firms, I am writing in regard to today's subcommittee hearing, titled, "The Future of Union Organizing." With a full quorum at the National Labor Relations Board (NLRB) and a recently confirmed Secretary of Labor, proponents of union organizing are demanding policy changes to increase declining membership.

As a result of their continued failure to pass the Employee Free Choice Act (EFCA), or "card check," organized labor and the Obama administration have shifted to administrative actions and rulemakings to meet their goals. The NLRB and the U.S. Department of Labor's (DOL) Office of Labor-Management Standards have been leading this effort. Two of the administration's proposals in particular are designed to work hand-in-glove to achieve EFCA's end goal of eliminating employer involvement in the union representation process. If allowed to take effect, these proposals will create an alarming imbalance in workplace labor relations that will give union organizers an unfair advantage, and infringe on employers' and employees' rights.

In a proposal first unveiled in 2011, the NLRB plans to authorize "ambush" elections, which would cut the timeframe between the filing of a union representation petition and the election itself from the current average of 38 days (which a top NLRB official referred to as "outstanding" and most employers accept as a reasonable amount of time) to as little as 10 days. This proposal is concerning to our members because the time after a representation petition is filed is crucial for employers to consult with qualified legal counsel and other advisors, comply with a multitude of paperwork and information-sharing requirements and, most importantly, exercise their right to communicate with employees about the advantages and disadvantages of being in a union. While this rule has been tied up in ongoing litigation, NLRB Chairman Mark Pearce has stated publicly that he is "determined to move forward."

The same week the NLRB issued its ambush elections proposal, DOL announced its own plans to transform workplace labor relations. DOL's proposal, known as "persuader" and slated to be finalized in November, severely narrows current rules that exempt reporting communications between attorneys (and other third party labor advisors) and their employer clients when they discuss labor issues. Employers' rights to free speech, freedom of association and legal counsel will be infringed, and employees' collective right to obtain balanced information to decide whether or not to be represented by a union will be significantly limited as well. Small businesses will be unquestionably discouraged from using outside legal assistance, and advisors, who will have to disclose relationships with other clients, will be more reluctant to offer assistance due to the unreasonable burdens imposed on them (and their clients) if they get involved.

66

ABC vehemently opposes any current or future policy or regulation that deprives employees of valuable, balanced information regarding the union representation process by obstructing employers' ability to communicate on the subject of union organizing. Viewed jointly, the NLRB and DOL proposals will rapidly speed up the union election process while simultaneously making it harder for employers to obtain expert advice.

ABC thanks the Subcommittee on Health, Employment, Labor and Pensions for holding today's hearing, and we look forward to assisting in any efforts to stop this assault on our industry's workplaces.

Sincerely,

Geoffrey G. Burr
Vice President, Government Affairs